DEVELOPING
A
STRONG MINDSET

DEVELOPING
A
STRONG MINDSET

500 MOTIVATIONAL QUOTES TO HELP YOU DEAL WITH:

- ❖ STRESS
- ❖ DEPRESSION
- ❖ SELF ESTEEM AND SELF CONFIDENCE
- ❖ ANXIETY
- ❖ LIFE
- ❖ LOVE AND HEARTBREAK
- ❖ CHANGE

AND MORE…

AARON KODUAH

DEVELOPING A STRONG MINDSET

First printing, 2018.

ISBN: 978-1-52723-097-2

Publisher

Aaron Koduah

United Kingdom

www.aaronkoduah.com

DEDICATED TO

MY LATE MOTHER

REV. HELENA KODUAH

MY INSPIRATION IN ALL GOOD TIMES AND BAD.

TABLE OF CONTENTS

INTRODUCTION

Life can be difficult sometimes and can push you to your absolute breaking point, it is full of uncertainties, challenges and unpredictable changes which you are forced to overcome, and it is essential on our journey's through life that we develop a strong mind set in order to do this.

Like many, I have been through many challenges in life, to the point of being at my lowest self. I too have spent countless hours, days and even weeks, comparing myself to others, leaving me feeling inadequate and absorbed in my own self-pity. During times like these, I would seek some form of guidance and understanding of my feelings using motivational quotes. I was able to seek snippets of words of wisdom that spoke directly to the mind, encouraging, motivating and uplifting my mood and sense of identity to a more positive place.

Once I realised the influential effect such words could have, I felt compelled to share. I have now been sharing motivational quotes for the past 17 years through social media, blogs and a motivational quotes page on my workplace intranet.

I hope my passion for such motivational teachings can bring the same understanding of one's feelings and emotions as they have to me. The contents of this book enabled me to build confidence and courage throughout my military career. I currently work within the rail industry, I decided to write motivational quotes on a 'Thought of the day' board at every station I worked at, this was to help motivate and uplift the mood of the public using the railways services. As a result, I have received countless of appreciations from complete strangers who have then gone on to share my thoughts on social media allowing the positivity to be shared further.

I highly recommend that you use the contents of this book as a tool in daily life, for example by randomly selecting a quote a day to focus on can allow you to be consistently developing a stronger mindset even when you feel no urgency to do so.

The quotes enclosed have been carefully selected to help you to develop a strong mindset to deal with any of the following life challenges; Change, Depression, Future, Life, Love and Heartbreak, Perseverance, Self Esteem and Self Confidence, Stress, Worry and Anxiety, Anger and Forgiveness.

I hope these teachings can bring you the same clarity and strength to tackle anything life throws at you.

Aaron Koduah

ABOUT THE AUTHOR

Aaron Koduah is a former soldier in the British Army. He served in operations within Afghanistan and travelled around Europe with the military. Following his service, he went on to achieve a degree in Accounting and Business management. After this accomplishment, he has been working within the railway industry. Through the utilisation of social media, blogs and motivational 'Thought of the day' boards within the working environment, the former soldier has been inspiring individuals to reach their full potential and beyond. Aaron Koduah is also a professional, certified Life Coach helping people build their self-confidence and self-esteem. You can obtain more information about the author from his blog www.aaronkoduah.com.

LOVE AND HEARTBREAK

The beauty of love is in sticking together as you initially planned with your partner, having the most exciting experiences of life together and sharing wonderful memories. As much as we have occurrences such as those, we also have experiences which end up with two loved up folks eventually getting torn apart- tragic!

These quotes will take you through the rigmarole of the surreal reality of love and give you a taste of the mishap, anguish and pain there is in the event of a heartbreak or letting go.

1

Change is painful. Growth is painful but,
nothing is as painful as staying stuck
somewhere you don't belong.

— *Mandy Hale.*

2

Time will decide who you meet in your life,
your heart decides who you want in your life,
and your behaviour decides
who stays in your life.

— *Unknown.*

3

Breakup hurts but, loosing someone who doesn't respect and
appreciate you is actually a gain not a loss.

— *Unknown.*

4

If you carry the bricks from your past relationship,
you end up building the same house.

— *Unknown.*

5

You can't force yourself to stop liking someone,
but you can tell yourself you deserve
better and try to move on.

— *Unknown.*

6

Pain makes you stronger. Tears makes you braver.
Heartbreak makes you wiser, so thank the past for a better
future.

— *Unknown.*

7

At some point you have to realize that they no longer care,
and that you're missing out on someone who does.

— *Unknown.*

8

You don't realize how badly you've been treated
until someone comes along and treat you
how you should be treated.

— *Unknown.*

9

Letting go doesn't mean you don't care about someone anymore. It's just realizing that the only person you really have control over is yourself.

— *Deborah Reber.*

10

Some people think that it's holding on that makes one strong, sometimes it's letting go.

— *Unknown.*

11

Breakups are painful, but not as painful as staying in a relationship that makes you unhappy.

— *Unknown.*

12

Closure happens right after you accept that letting go and moving on is more important than projecting a fantasy of how the relationship could have been.

— *Sylvester McNutt.*

13

Sometimes you just have to erase the messages, delete the numbers and move on. You don't have to forget who that person was to you, only accept that they aren't that person anymore.

— *Unknown.*

14

Dear Ex, I'm glad I had you as an example of what not to look for in the future.

— *Unknown.*

15

No relationship is ever a waste of time.
If it didn't bring you what you wanted,
it taught you what you don't want.

— *Unknown.*

16

To let go, you don't need strength. You need faith.

— *Unknown.*

17

The past is a place of reference not a place of residence.

— *Willie Jolley.*

18

No amount of guilt can change the past and no amount of worrying can change the future.

— *Umar Ibn Al-Khattab.*

19

It doesn't matter who hurt you or broke you down. What matters is who made you smile again.

— *Unknown.*

20

Everyone who is in your life is meant to be a part of your journey but, not all of them are meant to stay.

— *Unknown.*

21

Don't dwell too much on what went wrong. Instead,
focus on what to do next.

— *Denis Waitley.*

22

No matter how much it hurts now,
someday you will look back and realize your struggles
changed your life for better.

— *Unknown.*

23

When one door of happiness closes, another opens but,
often we look so long at the closed door that we do not
see the one that has been opened for us.

— *Helen Keller.*

24

We must be willing to let go of the life we've planned,
so as to have the life that is waiting for us.

— *Joseph Campbell.*

25

The only thing that makes it part of your life is that you keep thinking about it.

— *Anonymous.*

26

Never regret when you see your ex with someone else, because our parents taught us to give our used toys to the less fortunate.

— *Unknown.*

27

You may never be good enough for everybody, but you will always be the best for somebody.

— *Rihanna.*

28

Be strong enough to let go and wise enough to wait for what you deserve.

— *Unknown.*

29

You can't start a new chapter of your life if you keep re-reading the last one.

— Unknown.

30

Sometimes we need to forget some people from our past because of one simple reason, they just don't belong in our future.

— Unknown.

31

Forget it enough to get over it, remember it enough so it doesn't happen again.

— Unknown.

32

You know you are on the right track when you become uninterested in looking back.

— Unknown.

33

Your past has given you the strength and wisdom you have today, so celebrate it. Don't let it haunt you.

— *Unknown.*

34

Never regret- If it's good, it's wonderful. If it's bad, it's experience.

— *Anonymous.*

35

Regret doesn't remind us that we did badly,
it reminds us that we know that we could do better.

— *Kathryn Schultz.*

36

Don't let your past relationships ruin your future happiness, scars remind us of where we've been not where we are going.

— *Unknown.*

37

When you are too caught up on what happened in the past
you miss what's in front of you.

— *Unknown.*

38

Never regret anybody in your life,
because good people give us happiness and bad people
give us experience. Both are essentials in life.

— *Unknown.*

39

Sometimes we refuse to see how bad something is until it
destroys us.

— *Unknown.*

40

Don't let your happiness depend on something you may lose.

— *C.S Lewis.*

41

Never assume that someone loves you,
if they love you they'll tell you, show you or be with you.
Assumptions leads to heartbreak.

— *Sonya Parker.*

42

Sometimes what you are afraid of doing is the very thing
that will set you free.

— *Robert Tew.*

43

Don't feel sad over someone who gave up on you,
feel sorry for them because they gave up on someone
who would have never given up on them.

— *Frank Ocean.*

44

Let them miss you, sometimes when you are always
available they take you for granted because they
think you'll always stay.

— *Unknown.*

45

The first step to getting what you want is having the courage to get rid of what you don't want.

— Zig Ziglar.

46

Love is when the other person's happiness is more important than your own.

— Unknown.

47

Love is not about how many days,
weeks or months you've been together,
it's all about how much you love each other every day.

— Unknown.

48

Go for someone who is not only proud to have you but, will also take every risk just to be with you.

— Unknown.

49

Fall in love with someone who makes you question why you ever thought you would be better off alone.

— *Unknown.*

50

Sometimes what you're looking for comes when you are not looking.

— *Unknown.*

DEPRESSION

Every man is blessed with his peculiarity and he need to see that, the current menace in the world is everyone trying to be like someone else who they think is better than they are currently without knowing the phase which their admiree is currently in. We all want to be happy because we think our achievements can match up to our next neighbour's.

Living a life as this results in a wild goose chase for the kind of life your admiree has. What we fail to recognize is that the resultant effect of seemingly having made no progress in your new pursuit of the life of another demoralizes you, degrades your self-esteem and preaches to your mind "What am I living for if I cannot attain these goodies of life I see in my neighbour?"

The quotes present in this section seeks to alleviate you from this life and mentality!

51

Most people walk through life always giving up on themselves, one thing they always forget is that they won a greater race against millions before they got into this world, you were born a winner. Never give up. (The Race of Life).

— *Aaron Koduah.*

52

Sometimes when you're in a dark place,
you think you've been buried,
but you've actually been planted.

— *Christine Caine.*

53

The happiest people don't have the best of everything.
They just make the best of everything.

— *Anonymous.*

54

We are not given a good or a bad life.
We are given life and it's up to you to make it good or bad.

— *Unknown.*

55

Sometimes you must hurt in order to know, fall in order to grow, lose in order to gain, because life's greatest lessons are learned through pain.

— *Unknown.*

56

Rock bottom became the solid foundation on which I rebuilt my life.

— *J.K Rowling.*

57

Men are not prisoners of fate but, prisoners of their own minds.

— *Franklin D. Roosevelt.*

58

Stress, anxiety and depression are caused when we are living to please others.

— *Paulo Coelho.*

59

Happiness isn't about getting what you want all the time.
It's about loving what you have and being grateful for it.

— *Unknown.*

60

Tough times are like physical exercise.
You may not like it while you are doing it but,
tomorrow you will be stronger because of it.

— *Unknown.*

61

The strongest people are not those who show strength in
front of us but, those who win battles we know nothing
about.

— *Unknown.*

62

People cry not because they're weak.
It's because they've been strong for too long.

— *Johnny Depp.*

63

When something bad happens, you have three choices.
You can either let it define you, let it destroy you,
or you can let it strengthen you.

— *Unknown.*

64

Be miserable or motivate yourself. Whatever has to be done,
it's always your choice.

— *Wayne Dyer.*

65

We are all dealing with a challenge of some kind.
Some of us are just better at hiding it than others.

— *Unknown.*

66

Don't wait for everything to be perfect before you
decide to enjoy your life.

— *Joyce Meyer.*

67

Being happy doesn't mean everything is perfect. It means that you've decided to look beyond the imperfections.

— Unknown.

68

Happiness is not a destination. It is a mood,
it is not permanent. It comes and goes and if people thought that way then maybe people would find happiness more often.

— Unknown.

69

No, we don't always get what we want but consider this, there are people who will never have what you have right now.

— Unknown.

70

Happiness is a choice, not a result.
Nothing will make you happy until you choose to be happy. Your happiness will not come to you. It can only come from you.

— Ralph Marston.

71

Even a happy life cannot be without a measure of darkness,
and the word happy would lose its meaning if it
were not balanced with sadness.

— *Carl G. Jung.*

72

Remember that everyone you meet is afraid of something,
loves something and has lost something.
You are not alone, never give up on yourself.

— *Unknown.*

73

It's only when we truly know and understand that
we have a limited time on earth, and that we have no way of
knowing when our time is up, we will then begin to live each
day to the fullest, as if it was the only one we had.

— *Elisabeth Kubler-ross.*

74

Happiness is not determined by what's happening around you but rather, what's happening inside you. Most people depend on others to gain happiness but, the truth is, it always comes from within.

— Unknown.

75

You don't have a choice in what happens to you in life but, you always have the choice of how to respond to it.

— Aaron Koduah.

76

Happiness is not the absence of problems,

it's the ability to deal with them.

— Steve Maraboli.

77

It is not what they take away from you that counts. It's what you do with what you have left.

— Hubert Humphrey.

78

An entire sea of water can't sink a ship unless it gets inside the Ship. Similarly, the negativity of the world can't put you down unless you allow it to get inside you.

— Unknown.

79

Every situation in life is temporary.
So, when life is good, make sure you enjoy it.
And when life is not so good, remember that it will not last forever and better days are on the way.

— Jenni Young.

80

There is only one way to happiness and that is to cease worrying about things which are beyond the power of your will.

— Epictetus.

81

What seems to us as bitter trials are often blessings in disguise.

— Oscar Wilde.

82

Take time to be thankful for everything that you have.
You can always have more but, you could also have less.

— *Anonymous.*

83

Sometimes you have to get knocked down lower than you've
ever been, to rise up taller than you ever were.

— *Anonymous.*

84

Sometimes you have to accept the fact that certain things will
never go back to how they used to be.

— *Anonymous.*

85

You are not a failure until you believe you are.

— *Aaron Koduah.*

86

Our greatest glory is not in never failing but,
in rising every time we fall.

— *Confucius.*

87

Remember, sadness is always temporary. This too shall pass.

— *Chuck T. Falcon.*

88

Problems and disappointments shape and develop you into a
stronger person. Don't let them discourage you.

— *Aaron Koduah.*

89

What other people think of you is not your business.
If you start to make that your business,
you will be offended for the rest of your life.

— *Deepak Chopra.*

90

Stop hating yourself for everything you aren't and start loving yourself for everything you already are.

— *Unknown.*

91

Trying to get everyone to like you is a sign of mediocrity.

— *Oren Harari.*

92

A strong person is not the one who doesn't cry. A strong person is one who is quiet and sheds tears for a moment and then picks up the sword and fights again.

— *Unknown.*

93

What's broken can be mended. What hurts can be healed. And no matter how dark it gets; the Sun is going to rise again.

— *Unknown.*

94

You were giving this life because you are strong enough to live it.

— *Robin Sharma.*

95

Your time is limited so don't waste it living someone else's life. Don't be trapped by dogma, which is living with the results of other people's thinking. Don't let the noise of others' opinions drown out your own inner voice. And most important, have the courage to follow your heart and intuition. They somehow already know what you truly want to become. Everything else is secondary.

— *Steve Jobs.*

96

You were not born a winner, and you were not born a loser. You are what you make yourself to be.

— *Lou Holtz.*

97

Always remember that your present situation is not your final destination. The best is yet to come.

— *Unknown.*

98

Nothing holds you back more than your insecurities, accept your past without regrets, handle your present with confidence and face your future without fear. Be proud of who you are.

— Unknown.

99

Maybe you have to know the darkness before you can appreciate the light.

— Madeline L'Engle.

100

Don't waste your time looking back on what you've lost. Move on, for life is not meant to be travelled backwards.

— Unknown.

LIFE

Life, what it brings in the present and what it will yet bring in the future is a progression many have not been able to understand which makes its maximization a reality which only a few have been able to touch. The various phases of life bring about various experiences, memorable moments and challenges but those who are able to make the most of life are those who choose to live life's moments one at a time.

You may go wrong in making plans for 5 years ahead, but you can't go wrong making the most of everything that comes your way in the present- living now in the now.

101

When you focus too much on the way of life and the success
of other people, you will always be unhappy.
Instead, focus on you, focus on who you want to be and
what makes you happy. Always remember, we all have
different starts in life.

— *Aaron Koduah.*

102

The best day of your life is the one which you decide your
life is your own. No apologies or excuses. No one to lean on,
rely on or blame. This is the day that your life really begins.

— *Bob Moawad.*

103

Life is the most difficult exam, many people fail because they
try to copy others, not realizing that we all have different
question paper.

— *Unknown.*

104

If we all threw our problems in a pile and saw everyone else's, we'd grab ours back.

— *Unknown.*

105

We have no choice of what colour we're born or who our parents are or whether we're rich or poor. But we do have the choice of what we do with our lives once we're here.

— *Mildred D. Taylor.*

106

The less you worry about what people think, the less complicated life becomes.

— *Unknown.*

107

There was a man who cried because he had no shoes, until he met a man with no legs. Appreciate what you have because someone will always have less than you have.

— *Unknown.*

108

No matter how good or bad your life is, wake up each morning and be thankful that you still have one.

— *Unknown.*

109

Beware of destination addiction, the idea that happiness is in the next place, next job, or with the next partner. Until you give up the idea that happiness is somewhere else, it will never be where you are.

— *Robert Holden.*

110

You were not given a good or bad life. You were given life, and it's up to you to make it good or bad.

— *Unknown.*

111

It's ironic how people accept, love and appreciate the beauty of different colours in nature but refuse to accept the diversities within their own human race.

— *Aaron Koduah.*

112

Do not regret getting older. It is a privilege denied to many.

— *Unknown.*

113

Don't wait for everything to get easier or better.
Life will always be complicated. Learn to be happy right
now. Otherwise, you will run out of time.

— *Unknown.*

114

Everybody hopes things will get better, but what they forget
is, the future doesn't get better by hope.
It gets better by plan and action.

— *Aaron Koduah.*

115

Be thankful for what you have. Your life, no matter how bad
you think it is, is someone else's fairy-tale.

— *Wale Ayeni.*

116

Every choice you make is creating your future. Choose wisely.

— *Unknown.*

117

When life's problems seem overwhelming, look around and see what other people are coping with, you may consider yourself fortunate.

— *Ann Landers.*

118

Always keep your expectations of people low, that way you suffer less disappointment.

— *Unknown.*

119

Never regret a day in your life, good days give happiness, bad days give experience, worst days give lessons, and best days give memories.

— *Unknown.*

120

You are not in this world to live up to other people's expectations, nor should you feel the world must live up to yours.

— Unknown.

121

Nothing is ever permanent in this world, not even our troubles.

— Charlie Chaplin.

122

Every test in our life makes us bitter or better,
every problem comes to break us or make us. The choice is ours whether we become victim or victor.

— Unknown.

123

Sometimes the person who tries to keep everyone happy is the most lonely person.

— Unknown.

124

In life, you can have more than you've got because you can become more than you are. But unless you change how you are, you will always get what you've got.

— *Unknown.*

125

Life is not the way it's supposed to be. It's the way it is. The way you deal with it is what makes the difference.

— *Unknown.*

126

What disappoints us the most in life, is the picture in our head of how it's supposed to be.

— *Unknown.*

127

Sometimes you will never know the value of a moment until it becomes a memory.

— *Dr. Seuss.*

128

We've all got stories to tell, we're all dealing with our own issues but what makes us all the same is that none of us are living this perfect life that everyone thinks we are.

— Rebecca Black.

129

Life is like photography, we develop from the negatives.

— Unknown.

130

Sometimes you have to let go of what's gone, appreciate what remains and look forward to what comes next.

— Unknown.

131

There comes a day when you realize turning the page is the best feeling in the world, because you realize there is so much more to the book than the page you were stuck on.

— Unknown.

132

Life is like a book. Some chapters sad, some happy and some exciting. But if you never turn the page, you will never know what the next chapter holds.

— Unknown.

133

Sometimes life doesn't turn out the way you expected or hoped. That doesn't mean you can't be happy. If you don't limit yourself to your first version of your life, there's always a bright future ahead.

— Unknown.

134

Life isn't meant to be easy. It's meant to be lived. Sometimes happy, other times rough. But with every up and down you learn lessons that make you strong.

— Unknown.

135

Very little is needed to make a happy life; it is all within yourself, in your way of thinking.

— Marcus Aurelius.

136

Anyone who lives within their means suffers from a lack of imagination.

— *Oscar Wilde.*

137

Sometimes things that hurt you most, teach you the greatest lessons of life.

—*Unknown.*

138

Life isn't about finding yourself. Life is about creating yourself.

— *George Bernard Shaw.*

139

Change your thoughts and you change your world.

— *Norman Vincent Peale.*

140

We are all different. Don't judge, understand instead.

— *Roy T. Bennett.*

141

You should never regret anything in life. If it's good, it's wonderful. If it's bad, it's experience.

— *Unknown.*

142

Never regret anything that has happened in your life, it cannot be changed, undone or forgotten so take it as a lesson learned and move on.

— *Unknown.*

143

I've learned that people will forget what you said, people will forget what you did but, people will never forget how you made them feel.

— *Maya Angelou.*

144

You are the driver of your own life. Don't let anyone steal your seat.

— *Unknown.*

145

Moving on is not about forgetting them, it's about learning how to live without them.

— *Unknown.*

146

Life is a compromise between your feelings and reality, at every stage, you have to quit your feelings and accept the reality.

— *Unknown.*

147

Change your thinking. Change your life, your thoughts create your reality. Practice positive thinking. Act the way you want to be and soon you will be the way you act.

— *Les Brown.*

148

The trick in life is learning how to deal with it.

— Helen Mirren.

149

Someone's opinion of you does not have to be your reality.

— Les Brown.

150

Life will only change when you become more committed to your dreams than you are to your comfort zone.

— Billy Cox.

SELF ESTEEM & SELF CONFIDENCE

Self Esteem and Self Confidence are subjects which are unconsciously kick-started from a young age but not adequately tackled from sibling rivalry, to high-school bullying, the feeling of being a loner in college etc.

Individuals have inferiority complex because they believe others are superior to them in areas to which they are lacking. Inferiority in beauty, body type, family wealth, having little or no friends and so on. All these end the very day you choose to love yourself, work on the areas where you need to and see yourself as a work in progress. Others may be better than you in certain areas of life but that shouldn't put you down from working on becoming a better person.

151

Confidence isn't walking into a room with your nose
in the air and thinking you are better than everyone else,
it's walking into a room and not having to compare yourself
to anyone else in the first place.

— *Unknown.*

152

When you depend on people to build you up,
they'll have the same power to break you down.
You don't need their validation to know your worth.

— *Unknown.*

153

Your value does not decrease based on someone's inability
to see your worth.

— *Unknown.*

154

Loving yourself naturally leads to increase in self-confidence.

— *Cassie Parks.*

155

You are as beautiful or as ugly as you believe you are.
You define your beauty. That's not a power anyone can have
over you.

— Unknown.

156

Love yourself, compliment yourself, build yourself up.
Remember, you are unique just like everyone else.

— Unknown.

157

Care about what other people think and you will always
be their prisoner.

— Lao Tzu.

158

The better you feel about yourself, the less you feel
the need to show off.

— Robert Hand.

159

I am not what has happened to me, I am what I chose to become.

— *Carl Jung.*

160

Self-worth comes from within, you can't give it to someone and you can't expect others to give it to you.

— *Unknown.*

161

Happiness is found when you stop comparing yourself to others.

— *Unknown.*

162

Confidence is not 'They will like me'. Confidence is I'll be fine if they don't.

— *Unknown.*

163

Don't let others define you. Don't let the past confine you. Take charge of your life with confidence and determination and there are no limits on what you can do or be.

— *Michael Josephson.*

164

Low self-confidence isn't a life sentence. Self-confidence can be learned, practiced, and mastered just like any other skill. Once you master it, everything in your life will change for the better.

— *Barrie Davenport.*

165

You can have anything you want if you are willing to give up the belief that you can't have it.

— *Dr. Robert Anthony.*

166

Whether you think you can or think you can't, you are right.

— *Henry Ford.*

167

The Start is what stops most people.

— *Don Shula.*

168

The man who has confidence in himself gains
the confidence of others.

— *Unknown.*

169

Confidence is something you create within yourself by
believing in who you are.

— *Unknown.*

170

Nothing builds self-esteem and self-confidence like
accomplishments.

— *Thomas Carlyle.*

171

Wanting to be someone else is a waste of the person you are.

— Marilyn Monroe.

172

I used to walk into a room full of people and wonder if they liked me, now I look around and wonder if I like them.

— Unknown.

173

Anything is possible once you believe you are worthy of achieving it.

— Jason Pockrandt.

174

It doesn't matter what people think about you, it's what you think about yourself which is the most important.

— Aaron Koduah.

175

Too many of us spend our youth unhappy with the way we look but, the reality is, that's when we are our most beautiful.

— *Unknown.*

176

Confidence is the key. If you don't believe in yourself, then nobody will.

— *Unknown.*

177

Never accept anything less than you deserve. Remember, you teach people how to treat you.

— *Unknown.*

178

Happiness is when you feel good about yourself without feeling the need for anyone else's approval.

— *Unknown.*

179

No one is perfect. Love yourself as you are and train hard to become the best version that you can be.

— Unknown.

180

Enjoy who you are. Don't hate yourself for what you aren't.

— Anonymous.

181

Never be bullied into silence. Never allow yourself to be made a victim. Accept no one's definition of your life, define yourself.

— Harvey Fierstein.

182

No one can make you feel inferior without your consent.

— Eleanor Roosevelt.

183

The courage to be, is the courage to accept oneself,
despite being unacceptable.

— Paul Tillich.

184

Because one believes in oneself, one doesn't try to convince
others. Because one is content with oneself, one doesn't need
others' approval. Because one accepts oneself,
the whole world accepts him or her.

— Lao Tzu.

185

To be yourself in a world that is constantly trying to make
you something else is the greatest accomplishment.

— Ralph Waldo Emerson.

186

Everybody is a genius but, if you judge a fish by its ability to
climb a tree, it will live its whole life believing that it is
stupid.

— Albert Einstein.

187

Personality can open doors but, only character can keep them open.

— *Elmer G. Letterman.*

188

Why are you trying so hard to fit in when you were born to stand out?

— *Ian Wallace.*

189

Once you have accepted your flaws, no one can use them against you.

— *Unknown.*

190

Don't rely on someone else for your happiness and self-worth. Only you can be responsible for that. If you can't love and respect yourself — no one else will be able to make that happen. Accept who you are completely, the good and the bad and make changes as YOU see fit, not because you think someone else wants you to be different.

— *Unknown.*

191

It's not what you are that's holding you back.
It's what you think you are not.

— Unknown.

192

Self-esteem comes from being able to define the world in
your own terms and refusing to abide by the judgments of
others.

— Unknown.

193

We are who we choose to be.

— Green Goblin.

194

Believe you can and you are half way there.

— Theodore Roosevelt.

195

To fall in love with yourself is the first secret to happiness.

— *Robert Morley.*

196

Low self-esteem is like driving through life with your hand brake on.

— *Maxwell Maltz.*

197

Self-respect, self-worth, and self-love, all start with self. Stop looking outside of yourself for your value.

— *Rob Liano.*

198

Make sure you don't start seeing yourself through the eyes of those who don't value you. Know your worth even if they don't.

— *Unknown.*

199

Low self-esteem involves imagining the worst that other people can think about you.

— *Roger Ebert.*

200

One of the greatest regrets in life is being what others would want you to be, rather than being yourself.

— *Shannon L. Alder.*

STRESS

From time to time, we strive to have fast career progressions and wanting to be the best in our activities. As much as wanting these things are good, it is important to note that your life is at the mercy of the healthy state of your mind.

The mind has the power to break down the whole body through conjuring thoughts that are not healthy for it. It's not the actual situations that we face that necessarily bring about stress and strain to us but the thought of the things going on in our life. Unhealthy thoughts are like a disease which feeds on a mind at its mercy.

201

When everything is going wrong and you feel like giving up, always remember that, there is someone going through worse and would willingly rather walk in your shoes.

— *Aaron Koduah.*

202

Be thankful for hard times in your life, try not to look at them as bad things but, as opportunities to grow and learn.

— *Unknown.*

203

Don't think that someone else is more blessed than you are, it's just that, we are blessed in different ways.

— *Unknown.*

204

You must live through the worst part of life, so you never take the best parts for granted.

— *Unknown.*

205

Life's problems wouldn't be called hurdles if there wasn't a way to get over them.

— *Unknown.*

206

Don't compare your chapter 1 to someone else's chapter 20. Focus on yourself.

— *Unknown.*

207

Failures are part of life. If you don't fail, you don't learn. If you don't learn, you'll never change.

— *Unknown.*

208

Never assume that you're stuck with the way things are. Life changes every single moment and so can you.

— *Unknown.*

209

If you can solve your problem, then what is the need of worrying? If you cannot solve it, then what is the use of worrying?

— *Shanti deva.*

210

Don't let a bad day make you feel like you have a bad life.

— *Unknown.*

211

Anyone can run away from problems but, working through problems, that's what makes you strong.

— *Unknown.*

212

You cannot please everybody. Whatever you do, there will be people who will criticize you, so just do what you believe is right and don't be distracted by criticisms.

— *Unknown.*

213

Don't compare your life to others.
There's no comparison between the Sun and the Moon,
they shine when it's their time.

— *Unknown.*

214

Whoever is trying to bring you down is already below you.

— *Unknown.*

215

Do not let what you cannot do interfere with
what you can do.

— *John Wooden.*

216

No matter how many mistakes you make or how slow you
progress, you are still way ahead of everyone who isn't trying.

— *Anthony Robbins.*

217

As for worrying about what other people might think – forget it. They aren't concerned about you. They're too busy worrying about what you and other people think of them.

— *Michael le Boeuf.*

218

Remember that stress does not come from what is going on in your life. It comes from the thoughts about what's going on in your life.

— *Andrew J. Bernstein.*

219

There is greatness in each one of us, just believe in your abilities. Never give up no matter what. Nothing is more exciting than looking back at your past and being proud of how far you've come.

— *Aaron Koduah.*

220

Instead of beating yourself up about something you can't do, take a moment to appreciate the things you can do.

— *Unknown.*

221

You can't please everyone, and you can't make everyone like you.

— Katie Courtice.

222

You don't need a day to start over, you only need a new mindset.

— Unknown.

223

Saying yes to happiness means learning to say no to the things and people that stress you out.

— Thelma Davis.

224

You can do anything but not everything.

— Unknown.

225

It all begins and ends in your mind. What you give power to, has power over you, only if you allow it.

— *Unknown.*

226

It is not primarily our physical self that limit us but rather, our mindset about our physical limits.

— *Ellen J. Langer.*

227

Only humans worry about the future, regret the past, and blame ourselves for the present.

— *Rick Hanson.*

228

The happiness of your life depends on the quality of your thoughts.

— *Unknown.*

229

Spend time with people who bring out the best in you not the stress in you.

— *Unknown.*

230

Focus on what to do next instead of worrying about what went wrong.

— *Unknown.*

231

Desire is a contract you make with yourself to be unhappy until you get what you want.

— *Naval Ravikant.*

232

You are always responsible for how you act, no matter how you feel.

— *Robert Tew.*

233

Stress comes from within, it is your reaction to circumstances, not the circumstances themselves.

— *Brian Tracy.*

234

Just because you are right, does not mean I am wrong. You just haven't seen life from my side.

— *Anonymous.*

235

Do your best and let the rest go. You can't be perfect, no matter how hard you try, so give yourself credit for making an effort, and try to stop stressing about the outcome.

— *Lori Deschene.*

236

Use your struggles and frustrations today to motivate you rather than annoy you. You are in control of the way you look at life. Be mindful.

— *Marcandangel.*

237

Stressing and complaining will change nothing.

Take action, make a change, and never look back.

.— Unknown.

238

Frustration and stress come from the way you react, not the way things are. Adjust your attitude, and the frustration and stress is gone.

— Unknown.

239

Life has many ways of testing a person's will, either by having nothing happen at all or by having everything happen all at once.

— Paulo Coelho.

240

A couple of years from now, everything you are stressing about won't even matter. Keep moving forward.

— Anonymous.

241

You can't control the wind, but you can adjust the sails.

— *Unknown.*

242

If we want to manage our stress, we must manage our emotions.

— *Erin Olivo.*

243

Just because one thing goes wrong doesn't mean your life is ruined. Stay positive.

— *Unknown.*

244

If you want to test your memory, try to recall what you were worrying about one year ago today.

— *E. Joseph Cossman.*

245

Hope but never expect. Look forward but never wait.

— *Unknown.*

246

No matter the situation, never let your emotions overpower your intelligence.

— *Unknown.*

247

If you can't do anything about it, then let it go. Don't be a prisoner to things you can't change.

— *Tony Gaskins.*

248

Do not get upset with people or situations, both are powerless without your reaction.

— *Unknown.*

249

The less you respond to negative people, the more peaceful
your life will become.

— Unknown.

250

The secret to living the life of your dreams is to start living
the life of your dreams today, in every little
way you possibly can.

— Mike Dooley.

CHANGE

The fear of starting over or going on a new path has robbed many from the benefits of change. Change in direction has many at times been seen in the negative light while neglecting the pros which it holds. It is impossible to expect to end at destination A while taking the route of destination B.

What stops many from making the change that they most desire is because of the focus on the unpleasantness accompanied with change. We must try to see that although change would sting you, its eventual benefit outweighs the cons which you have highlighted mostly in your mind and sometimes on paper.

251

There are two primary choices in life; to accept conditions as they exist or accept the responsibility for changing them.

— *Dr. Denis Waitley.*

252

People change for two reasons, they have learned a lot, or they have been hurt too many times.

— *Unknown.*

253

It's amazing how your life changes when you embrace the reality that you're better than the life you've settled for.

— *Dr. Steve Maraboli.*

254

Don't be afraid to change, you may lose something good but, you may gain something better.

— *Unknown.*

255

Life goes on whether you choose to move on and take a chance in the unknown or stay behind locked in the past thinking of what could have been.

— *Unknown.*

256

The beautiful thing about life is that you can always change, grow and get better. You aren't defined by your past. You aren't your mistakes.

— *Unknown.*

257

Find the courage to let go of what you can't change.

— *Unknown.*

258

We change our behaviour when the pain of staying the same becomes greater than the pain of changing. Consequences give us the pain that motivates us to change.

— *Henry Cloud.*

259

If you're searching for that one person that will change your life, look in the mirror.

— *Unknown.*

260

You are who you are and what you are because of what has gone into your mind. You can change who you are and what you are by changing what goes into your mind.

— *Zig Ziglar.*

261

Progress is impossible without change, and those who cannot change their minds cannot change anything.

— *George Bernard Shaw.*

262

One reason why people resist change is because they focus on what they have to give up, instead of what they have to gain.

— *Unknown.*

263

You cannot change your destination overnight, but you can change your direction overnight.

— Jim Rohn.

264

It is not the strongest species that survive, nor the most intelligent, but the ones who are most responsive to change.

— Charles Darwin.

265

Old ways won't open new doors.

— Unknown.

266

We cannot become what we were born to be by remaining what we are.

— Max Depree.

267

If you want to live a happy life, tie it to a goal,
not to people or objects.

— *Albert Einstein.*

268

Though no one can go back and make a brand-new start,
anyone can start from now and make a brand-new ending.

— *Carl Bard.*

269

When we are no longer able to change a situation,
we are challenged to change ourselves.

— *Viktor E. Frankl.*

270

Just when I think I have learned the way to live life, life
changes.

— *Hugh Prather.*

271

Any change, even a change for the better is always accompanied by drawbacks and discomfort.

— *Arnold Bennett.*

272

Change is not pleasant, but change is constant. Only when we change and grow, we'll see a world we never know.

— *Unknown.*

273

Sometimes there are things in life that aren't meant to stay. Sometimes change may not be what we want. Sometimes change is what we need.

— *Unknown.*

274

There are three solutions to every problem: accept it, change it, or leave it. If you can't accept it, change it. If you can't change it, leave it.

— *Unknown.*

275

People who can change and change again are so much more reliable and happier than those who can't.

— *Stephen Fry.*

276

Our only security is our ability to change.

— *John Lilly.*

277

You cannot change your life until you change something you do daily. The secret of your success is found in your daily routine.

— *Unknown.*

278

Sometimes the things we can't change end up changing us.

— *Unknown.*

279

The goal isn't to get rid of all your negative thoughts and feelings. The goal is to change your response to them.

— *Unknown.*

280

Either you run the day, or the day runs you.

— *Jim Rohn.*

281

You're always one decision away from a totally different life.

— *Unknown.*

282

You can't stop the waves, but you can learn to surf.

— *John Kabat-Zin.*

283

They always say time changes,
but you actually have to change them yourself.

— *Andy Warhol.*

284

Your choices of action may be limited, but your choices of thought are not.

— *Unknown.*

285

Change can be scary, but you know what's scarier? Allowing fear to stop you from Growing, Evolving and Progressing.

— *Mandy Hale.*

286

Your life does not get better by chance. It gets better by change.

— *Jim Rohn.*

287

If you don't like something, change it, if you can't change it, change the way you think about it.

— *Mary Engelbreit.*

288

Every story has an end. But in life, every ending is a new beginning.

— *Unknown.*

289

When life changes to be harder, change yourself to be stronger.

— *Unknown.*

290

The real winners in life are the people who look at every situation with an expectation that they can make it work or make it better.

— *Unknown.*

291

Change is the law of life, and those who look only to the past or present are certain to miss the future.

— *John F. Kennedy.*

292

Don't try to overhaul your life overnight. Instead, focus on making one small change at a time. Over time, those small changes will add up to big transformation. Don't give up.

— *Unknown.*

293

Conformity is the jailer of freedom and enemy of growth.

— *John F. Kennedy.*

294

Change the changeable, accept the unchangeable, and remove yourself from the unacceptable.

— *Denis Waitley.*

295

Change only takes place through action, not through meditation and prayer alone.

— *Dalai Lama.*

296

When looking back doesn't interest you anymore,
you are doing something right.

— Unknown.

297

The beauty of life is, while we can't undo what is done, we
can see it, understand it, learn from it and change.

— Unknown.

298

I don't regret the things I've done, I regret the things I didn't
do when I had the chance.

— Unknown.

299

In order to change your life, you must change your thoughts.

— Denzel Washington.

300

Worrying about something you can't change will forever be the biggest waste of your time.

— Unknown.

FACING THE FUTURE

The future is a place where individuals desire to be successful but have little or no know-how on how it will all happen. Some fellows have retired in making efforts and succumbed to the mind-set of thinking whatever will be, will be.

To get the desired result out of life, you must choose to be deliberate about your decisions and steps towards life because no one knows what will become of him in the days to come but when proper preparation meets opportunity, success is inevitable as said by Zig Ziglar.

301

We become, what we think about.

— *Earl Nightingale.*

302

A man should look for what is, and not for what he thinks should be.

— *Albert Einstein.*

303

A year from now you may wish you had started today.

— *Karen Lamb.*

304

Your present circumstances do not determine your future success.

— *Aaron Koduah.*

305

Accept responsibility for your life. Know that it is you who will get you where you want to go, no one else.

— Les Brown.

306

Choose the job you love, and you will never have to work a day in your life.

— Confucius.

307

The will to succeed is important, but what's more important is the will to prepare.

— Bobby Knight.

308

If you don't build your dream, someone will hire you to build theirs.

— Tony Gaskins Jr.

309

Be thankful for what you are now and keep fighting for what you want to be tomorrow.

— *Unknown.*

310

Don't wait until everything is just right. It will never be perfect. There will always be challenges, obstacles and less than perfect conditions. So, what. Get started now. With each step you take, you will grow stronger and stronger, more and more skilled, more and more self-confident and more and more successful.

— *Mark Victor Hansen.*

311

Experience life in all possible ways good-bad, bitter, sweets, dark, light, summer, winter. Experience all the dualities. Don't be afraid of experience, because the more experience you have, the more mature you become.

— *Osho.*

312

I am not a product of my circumstances.
I am a product of my decisions.

— *Stephen Covey.*

313

If you love life, don't waste time, for time is what life is made up of.

— *Bruce lee.*

314

There are two great days in a person's life, the day we are born and the day we discover why.

— *William Barclay.*

315

If you are born poor it's not your mistake but, if you die poor, it's your mistake.

— *Bill Gates.*

316

In order to succeed, your desire for success should be greater than your fear of failure.

— *Bill Cosby.*

317

It is in your moments of decision that your destiny is shaped.

— *Anthony Robbins.*

318

If you wait, all that happens is you get older.

— *Larry McMurtry.*

319

It's never too late to be what you might have been.

— *George Elliot.*

320

Never allow waiting to become a habit. Live your life and take risks. Life is happening now.

— *Paulo Coelho.*

321

If you don't make the time to work on creating the life you want, you're eventually going to be forced to spend a LOT of time dealing with a life you DON'T want.

— *Kevin Ngo.*

322

Incredible change happens in your life when you decide to take control of what you do have power over instead of craving control over what you don't.

— *Steve Maraboli.*

323

One day you will wake up and there won't be any more time to do the things you've always wanted. Do it now.

— *Paulo Coelho.*

324

Don't expect to see a change if you don't make one.

— *Unknown.*

325

Right now, you are looking at the results of your past creations and right now, how you feel is creating your future.

— Odille Rault.

326

Some people dream of success whilst others wake up and work hard at it.

— Unknown.

327

Success is not the key to happiness. Happiness is the key to success. If you love what you are doing, you will be successful.

— Herman Cain.

328

Almost every successful person begins with two beliefs: the future can be better than the present, and I have the power to make it so.

— David Brooks.

329

The best way to predict the future is to create it.

— *Abraham Lincoln.*

330

If you look at what you have in life, you'll always have more.
If you look at what you don't have in life,
you'll never have enough.

— *Oprah Winfrey.*

331

The difference between a successful person and others is not
a lack of strength, not a lack of knowledge but rather,
in a lack of will.

— *Vince Lombardi.*

332

The great thing in the world is not so much where we stand,
as in what direction we are moving.

— *Oliver W Holmes.*

333

The mind is everything. What you think you become.

— *Buddha.*

334

The only person you are destined to become is the person you decide to be.

— *Ralph Waldo Emerson.*

335

Time is all you have, and you may find one day that you have less than you think.

— *Randy Pausch.*

336

Try not to become a man of success, but, rather try to become a man of value.

— *Albert Einstein.*

337

If you wait to do everything you're sure it's right,
you'll probably never do much of anything.

—Unknown.

338

Two sure ways to fail. Think and never do or do and never
think.

— Zig Ziglar.

339

Where you end up doesn't depend on where you start, it
depends on which direction you choose to take from where
you currently stand.

— Kevin Ngo.

340

You don't have to be great to start but, you have to start to
be great.

— John C. Maxwell.

341

You don't have to see the whole staircase, just take the first step.

— *Martin Luther King Jr.*

342

You got to get out there, take risks, put in the work, and not be afraid to fail. The longer you wait, the less opportunities you'll have to try again if you do fail. The longer you put off pursuing your dreams, the less time you'll have to enjoy your success if you succeed. Time doesn't stop for any of us.

— *Kevin Ngo.*

343

You have to expect things of yourself before you can do them.

— *Michael Jordan.*

344

Your current life is the result of your previous choices, if you want something different, begin to choose differently.

— *Joe Tichio.*

345

The trouble for most people is they don't decide to get wealthy, they just dream about it.

— *Michael Masterson.*

346

If you always do what you've always done, you'll always get what you've always got.

— *Steven Hayes.*

347

Curiosity is the key to creativity.

— *Akio Morita.*

348

Go confidently in the direction of your dreams. Live the life you have imagined.

— *Henry David Thoreau.*

349

The depth of your struggle will determine the height of your success.

— *R. Kelly.*

350

Look closely at the present you are constructing, it should look like the future you are dreaming.

— *Alice Walker.*

PERSEVERANCE

Never quit after your first few trials in your field of engagement. We all want that scheme that makes us rich at the snap of a finger but what happens when you have to persevere for a year before you achieve your goal. You never know how close you are to success if you give up just before you've attained it.

At every point where giving up feels like the easiest and next best thing to do, have a rethink on what success you could attain if only you used the towel as a wipe rather than throwing it in, in defeat.

351

Strength does not come from winning. Your struggles develop your strengths. When you go through hardships and decide not to surrender, that is strength.

— Arnold Schwarzenegger.

352

Just because you are taking longer than others doesn't mean you're a failure. Keep going.

— Anonymous.

353

It's going to be hard. But hard is not impossible.

— Unknown.

354

If you can't fly, then run, if you can't run, then walk, if you can't walk, then crawl, but whatever you do, you have to keep moving forward.

— Martin Luther King Jr.

355

Good things come to those who wait but, better things come to those who go out and get them.

— Anonymous.

356

If you fail to rise up for something, you fall for anything.

— Aaron Koduah.

357

The number one reason why people quit is because they look how far they've got to go, not how far they've come.

— Unknown.

358

Success doesn't just come and find you, you have to go out there and get it.

— Unknown.

359

Never give up on a dream just because of the time it will take to accomplish it. The time will pass anyway.

— *Earl Nightingale.*

360

Take risks, if you win you will be happy, if you lose, you will be wise.

— *Unknown.*

361

The level of your input determines the level of your output.

— *Aaron Koduah.*

362

Start where you are, use what you have, do what you can.

— *Arthur Ashe.*

363

If you don't try, you might never know that what you've always perceived as difficult might be easier than you think.

— *Aaron Koduah.*

364

Giving up on your goal because of one set back is like slashing your other three tyres because you got a flat.

— Unknown.

365

What you do every day matters more than what you do once in a while.

— *Gretchen Rubin.*

366

We must all suffer from one of two pains: the pain of discipline or the pain of regret. The difference is discipline weighs ounces while regret weighs tons.

— *Jim Rohn.*

367

He who is not courageous enough to take risks will accomplish nothing in life.

— *Muhammad Ali.*

368

Strength and growth come only through continues effort and struggle.

— *Napoleon Hill.*

369

It's not what we do once in a while that shapes our lives. It's what we do consistently.

— *Anthony Robbins.*

370

Many of life's failures are experienced by people who did not realize how close they were to success when they gave up.

— *Thomas Edison.*

371

Do not pray for an easy life, pray for the strength to
endure a difficult one.

— *Bruce Lee.*

372

The difference between a successful person and others is not
a lack of strength, not a lack of knowledge, but, rather a lack
of will.

— *Vince Lombardi.*

373

It does not matter how slowly you go, so long as you do not
stop.

— *Confucius.*

374

Every day do something that will inch you closer
to a better tomorrow.

— *Doug Firebaugh.*

375

Life is like riding a bicycle. To keep your balance,
you must keep moving.

— *Albert Einstein.*

376

Challenges are what make life interesting and overcoming
them is what makes life meaningful.

— *Joshua J. Marine.*

377

It's not about how bad you want it, it is about how hard you
are willing to work for it.

— *Unknown.*

378

The hardest battle you will ever have to fight is between who
you are now and who you want to be.

— *Unknown.*

379

If you don't sacrifice for what you want, what you want
becomes the sacrifice.

— Unknown.

380

Obstacles can't stop you, problems can't stop you, most of
all, other people can't stop you. The only one who stops you
is yourself.

— Unknown.

381

I am a slow walker. But, I never walk back.

— Abraham Lincoln.

382

Obstacles are put in your way to see if what you want is
really worth fighting for.

— Unknown.

383

There are no short cuts. Work hard, be patient, consistent and never give up.

— **Unknown.**

384

Don't quit. Suffer now and live the rest of your life as a champion.

— *Muhammad Ali.*

385

You can have more than you've got because you can become more than you are. But, unless you change how you are, you will always have what you've got.

— *Unknown.*

386

If you are not willing to go beyond your current circumstances, you will never grow.

— *Aaron Koduah.*

387

It's better to cross the line and face the consequences than to just stare at the finish line for the rest of your life.

— *Unknown.*

388

Excuses are the nails used to build the house of failure.

— *Jim Rohn.*

389

The past is your lesson, the present is your gift. The future is your motivation.

— *Unknown.*

390

Success is not final, failure is not fatal, it is the courage to continue that counts.

— *Winston Churchill.*

391

No one succeeds without effort, those who succeed owe
their success to perseverance.

— *Ramana Maharshi.*

392

The difference between the impossible and the possible lies
in a person's determination.

— *Tommy Lasorda.*

393

With ordinary talent and extraordinary perseverance,
all things are attainable.

— *Thomas Fowell Buxton.*

394

We can do anything we want to do if we stick to it long
enough.

— *Helen Keller.*

395

I've failed over and over and over again in my life and that is why I succeed.

— Michael Jordan.

396

You aren't going to find anybody that's going to be successful without making a sacrifice and without perseverance.

— Lou Holtz.

397

As long as a man stands in his own way, everything seems to be in his way.

— Ralph Waldo Emerson.

398

You can find inspiration from others, but determination is solely your responsibility.

— Unknown.

399

The man who moves a mountain begins by carrying away small stones.

— Confucius.

400

Just because you fail once doesn't mean you're going to fail at everything.

— Marilyn Monroe.

WORRY & ANXIETY

Worry is the safe place of every individual who chickens out of facing his current challenge head-on and wants to wallow in self-pity and "had I known". Amazingly, worry and anxiety begin where the mind has made itself to believe that it can do nothing- a lie!

Action on the other hand is a kinetic force which displaces worry like it never existed sparked up by saying to yourself "I can overcome this". Do not let worry and anxiety get a hold of you as it has the ability to paralyze your mind like an epidemic if not quarantined.

401

The greatest mistake you can make in life is to be continually fearing you will make one.

— Elbert Hubbard.

402

Worrying does not take away tomorrow's troubles, it takes away today's peace.

— Unknown.

403

You may not control all the events that happen to you, but you can decide not to be reduced by them.

— Maya Angelou.

404

When you're different, sometimes you don't see the millions of people who accept you for what you are. All you notice is the person who doesn't.

— Jodi Picoult.

405

It's a shame when the things in your mind and in your heart never reach your lips.

— *Unknown.*

406

Nothing diminishes anxiety faster that action.

— *Unknown.*

407

Although anxiety is part of life. Do not let it control you.

— *Paulo Coelho.*

408

When I accept myself, I am freed from the burden of needing you to accept me.

— *Dr. Steve Maraboli.*

409

Shyness has a strange element of narcissism, a belief that how we look, how we perform, is truly important to other people.

— *Andre Dubus.*

410

Thinking will not overcome fear but, action will.

— *W. Clement Stone.*

411

When you are feeling shy, you are just thinking of all the things that people might say about you.

— *Unknown.*

412

The greatest prison people live in is the fear of what other people think.

— *David Icke.*

413

You're not going to master the rest of your life in one day. Just relax. Master the day. Then keep doing that every day.

— Unknown.

414

Worrying is like sitting in a rocking chair. It gives you something to but, it doesn't take you anywhere.

— English Proverb.

415

You don't have to control your thoughts. You just have to stop letting them control you.

— Unknown.

416

Do not let your difficulties fill you with anxiety, after all, it is only in the darkest nights that stars shine more brightly.

— Unknown.

417

When you change the way you look at things, the things you look at change.

— Wayne Dyer.

418

Anxiety isn't something that goes away, it's something you learn to control.

— Unknown.

419

You don't get to choose how you are going to die or when. But you can decide how you're going to live now.

— Joan Baez.

420

Worry does nothing but steal your joy and keep you very busy doing nothing.

— Unknown.

421

Anxiety is nothing but repeatedly re-experiencing failure in advance. What a waste.

— *Seth Godin.*

422

Don't let your fear of what could happen make nothing happen.

— *Unknown.*

423

It's not the future that you're afraid of. It's repeating the past that makes you anxious.

— *Unknown.*

424

Our anxiety does not come from thinking about the future, but from wanting to control it.

— *Khalil Gibran.*

425

Once you become fearless, life becomes limitless.

— *Unknown.*

426

Most of the things you worry about never happens.

— *Unknown.*

427

The day you stop worrying will be the first day of your new life. Anxiety takes you in circles, trust in yourself and become free.

— *Leon Brown.*

428

It is through falling down that we learn how to stand up again. It is through adversity that we gather our strengths to live the life we want and pursue our dreams.

— *Unknown.*

429

Stop being afraid of what could go wrong and start focusing on what could go right.

— *Unknown.*

430

The reason people find it so hard to be happy is that they always see the past better than it was and the present worse than it is.

— *Unknown.*

431

Don't think too much. You'll create a problem that wasn't even there in the first place.

— *Unknown.*

432

Fear is interest paid on a debt you may not owe.

— *Unknown.*

433

Anything is possible when you stop believing it is impossible. Life doesn't provide warranties and guarantees, it only provides possibilities and opportunities for those who dare to make best use of it.

— *Unknown.*

434

No amount of anxiety makes any difference to anything that is going to happen.

— *Allan Watts.*

435

Fear only becomes powerful when you give it your power.

— *Unknown.*

436

What you're worrying about probably won't ever happen.

— *Unknown.*

437

Overthinking is not going to make anything better. Focus on what you can control, the possibilities not the problems and let the rest go.

— Unknown.

438

You can conquer almost any fear if you will only make up your mind to do so. For remember, fear doesn't exist anywhere except in the mind.

— Dale Carnegie.

439

Don't believe every worried thought you have. Worried thoughts are notoriously inaccurate.

— Renee Jain.

440

The less you worry, the less complicated life becomes.

— Unknown.

441

He who fears what he shall suffer, already suffers what he fears.

— *Unknown.*

442

Look for something positive in every day. Even if some days you have to look a little harder.

— *Unknown.*

443

Sometimes you have to stop worrying, wondering and doubting. Have faith that things will work out, maybe not how you planned, but just how it's meant to be.

— *Unknown.*

444

What worries you, masters you.

— *Haddon W. Robinson.*

445

Someday everything will make perfect sense. So, for now laugh at the confusion, smile through the tears, and keep reminding yourself that everything happens for a reason.

— *John Mayer.*

446

If you want to be happy, do not dwell in the past, do not worry about the future, focus on living fully in the present.

— *Roy T. Bennett.*

447

Whatever is going to happen will happen, whether we worry or not.

— *Ana Monnar.*

448

If you worry about something that you have no control over, or can absolutely do nothing about, then you are wasting your time, energy and emotion.

— *Byron Pulsifer.*

449

Nothing can bring you peace but yourself.

— *Ralph Waldo Emerson.*

450

Maybe it's not always about trying to fix something broken.
Maybe it's about starting over and creating something better.

— *Unknown.*

ANGER & FORGIVENESS

Some say it's genetic while others say it's a temperament, but I say it's a choice. Anger never does any good but leaves you with words and actions you wish you never said nor did. The less angry you choose to be, the happier your life would turn out and the more you appreciate the uniqueness of others.

Forgiveness is not a show of weakness but a pointer that you are in control of your mind and yourself, with no one being able to distort your emotional peace as they will.

451

A moment of patience in a moment of anger can save you a hundred moments of regret.

— *Unknown.*

452

Be careful with your words. Once they are said, they can be only forgiven, not forgotten.

— *Unknown.*

453

The more anger towards the past you carry in your heart, the less capable you are of loving in the present.

— *Unknown.*

454

Holding a grudge doesn't make you strong, it makes you bitter. Forgiving doesn't make you weak, it sets you free.

— *Unknown.*

455

Speak when you are angry, and you will make the best speech you will ever regret.

— *Ambrose Bierce.*

456

People who fly into a rage always make a bad landing.

— *Will Rogers.*

457

Explain your anger instead of expressing it, and you will find solutions instead of arguments.

— Dr. Steve Maraboli.

458

You will not be punished for your anger, you will be punished by your anger.

— *Buddha.*

459

Forgive people in your life even those who are not sorry for their actions. Holding on to anger only hurts you not them.

— *Unknown.*

460

Anybody can become angry, that is easy but, to be angry with the right person and to the right degree and at the right time and for the right purpose and in the right way, that is not within everybody's power and is not easy.

— *Aristotle.*

461

Don't do something permanently stupid just because you are temporarily upset.

— *Unknown.*

462

Life is short, live it. Love is rare, grab it. Anger is bad, let go of it. Fear is a mind killer, face it. Memories are sweet, cherish them.

— *Unknown.*

463

A lot of problems in the world would disappear if we talk to each other instead of about each other.

— Unknown.

464

Holding onto anger is like grasping a hot coal with the intent of throwing it at someone else, you are the one who gets burned.

— Buddha.

465

The truly strong people do not stoop to anger.

— Confucius.

466

The one that angers you controls you. Don't give anyone that power, especially the one who does it intentionally.

— Unknown.

467

People won't have time for you if you are always angry or complaining.

— *Stephen Hawking.*

468

Anger is a feeling that makes your mouth work faster than your mind.

— *Evan Esar.*

469

If we really want to love, we must learn how to forgive.

— *Mother Teresa.*

470

When you forgive, you heal. When you let go, you grow.

— *Unknown.*

471

Forgive others not because they deserve forgiveness, but because you deserve peace.

— *Unknown.*

472

Sometimes you forgive people because you still want them in your life.

— *Unknown.*

473

Forgive all who have offended you, not for them, but for yourself.

— *Harriet Nelson.*

474

Let no man pull you low enough to hate him.

— *Martin Luther King Jr.*

475

Forgiving someone isn't approving how they wronged you rather, it's no longer allowing their wrong to define you.

— *Unknown.*

476

There are two things a person should never be angry at, what they can help and what they cannot.

— *Plato.*

477

Anger doesn't solve anything. It builds nothing, but it can destroy everything.

— *Laurence Douglas Wilder.*

478

Mistakes are always forgivable if one has the courage to admit them.

— *Bruce Lee.*

479

Life becomes easier when you learn to accept an apology you never got

— Robert Brault.

480

Anger makes you smaller, while forgiveness forces you to grow beyond what you were.

— Cherie Carter-Scott.

481

Sometimes letting things go is an act of far greater power than defending or hanging on.

— Eckhart Tolle.

482

Don't hold on to Anger, Hurt or Pain. They steal your energy and keep you from Love.

— Unknown.

483

A smart person knows what to say, a wise person knows whether to say it or not.

— *Unknown.*

484

Forgiving someone isn't approving how they wronged you, rather it's no longer allowing their wrong to define you.

— *Unknown.*

485

Everyone makes mistakes. If you can't forgive others, don't expect others to forgive you.

— *Unknown.*

486

You will know that forgiveness has begun when you recall those who hurt you and feel the power to wish them well.

— *Lewis B. Smedes.*

487

There is no love without forgiveness, and there is no forgiveness without love.

— Bryant H. McGill.

488

When you forgive, you in no way change the past but you sure do change the future.

— Bernard Meltzer.

489

Let go of the grudges of yesterday and hold on to the hope of tomorrow.

— Unknown.

490

When a deep injury is done to us, we never heal until we forgive.

— Nelson Mandela.

491

Forgiveness is not an occasional act, it is a constant attitude.

— *Martin Luther King Jr.*

492

An eye for an eye. And the whole world would be blind.

— *Kahlil Gibran.*

493

The decision to forgive touches you to your very core, to who you are as a human being.

— *Robert Enright.*

494

The weak can never forgive. Forgiveness is the attribute of the strong.

— *Mahatma Gandhi.*

495

Forgive. Because none of us are perfect.

— *Unknown.*

496

You cannot travel back in time to fix your mistakes, but you can learn from them and forgive yourself for not knowing better.

— *Leon Brown.*

497

I believe forgiveness is the best form of love in any relationship. It takes a strong person to say they're sorry and an even stronger person to forgive.

— *Yolanda Hadid.*

498

Darkness cannot drive out darkness; only light can do that. Hate cannot drive out hate; only love can do that.

— *Martin Luther King, Jr.*

499

Forgiveness says you are given another chance to make a new beginning.

— Desmond Tutu.

500

Don't live your life with anger and hate in your heart. You'll only be hurting more than the people you hate.

— Unknown.

REFERENCES

1. **Mandy Hale** is the Author of a book known as The Single Woman which is widely recognized around the world.

2. **Unknown.**

3. **Unknown.**

4. **Unknown.**

5. **Unknown.**

6. **Unknown.**

7. **Unknown.**

8. **Unknown.**

9. **Deborah Reber** is a young adult fiction and non-fiction writer. She previously worked in children's television. She is the author of several books including a book titled: In Their Shoes.

10. **Unknown.**

11. **Unknown.**

12. **Sylvester McNutt** is a speaker, a storyteller and an

international best-selling Author with books including A Path to Deep Healing, Lust for Life, The Dear Queen Journey etc.

13. **Unknown.**

14. **Unknown.**

15. **Unknown.**

16. **Unknown.**

17. **Willie Jolley** is a world-renowned speaker, singer, author and media personality. In 1999 he was named One of the Outstanding Five Speakers in the World and Motivational / Inspirational Speaker of The Year by the 175,000 members of Toastmasters International.

18. **Umar Ibn Al-Khattab** was one of the most powerful and influential Muslim caliphs in history. He was a senior companion of the Prophet Muhammad. He succeeded Abu Bakr as the second caliph of the Rashidun Caliphate on 23 August 634.

19. **Unknown.**

20. **Unknown.**

21. **Denis Waitley** is an American motivational speaker, writer and consultant. He has been recognized as the best-selling author of the audio series, The Psychology of Winning and books such as Seeds of Greatness and The Winner's Edge. Waitley has been inducted into the

International Speakers' Hall of Fame.

22. Unknown.

23. Helen Keller was an American author, political activist, and lecturer. She was the first deaf-blind person to earn a Bachelor of Arts degree.

24. Joseph Campbell was an American Professor of Literature at Sarah Lawrence College who worked in comparative mythology and comparative religion. His work covers many aspects of the human experience.

25. Anonymous.

26. Unknown.

27. Rihanna is a Barbadian singer, songwriter, actress, and businesswoman. Born in Saint Michael Barbados and raised in Bridgetown.

28. Unknown.

29. Unknown.

30. Unknown.

31. Unknown.

32. Unknown.

33. Unknown.

34. Anonymous.

35. Kathryn Schultz is an American journalist and author, and the former book critic for New York magazine. She joined The New Yorker as a staff writer in 2015.

36. **Unknown.**

37. **Unknown.**

38. **Unknown.**

39. **Unknown.**

40. **C. S. Lewis** was a British novelist, poet, academic, medievalist, literary critic, essayist, lay theologian, broadcaster, lecturer, and Christian apologist. He is best known for his works of fiction, especially The Screwtape Letters, The Chronicles of Narnia, and The Space Trilogy.

41. **Sonya Parker** is an author of Letting go of Mr Wrong.

42. **Robert Tew** has been Chairman at Newcastle Knights Limited since April 11, 2011 and its Director since April 2008. Mr. Tew served as Director of Tew Property Consultants. He was Committee Member of Once a Knight Old Boys Club Inc.

43. **Frank Ocean** is an American singer, songwriter, rapper, record producer and photographer. Known for his idiosyncratic musical style. Ocean first embarked on a career as a ghost-writer, and in 2010 he became a member of hip hop collective Odd Future.

44. **Unknown.**

45. **Zig Ziglar** was an American author, salesman, and motivational speaker. Zig Ziglar was born in Coffee County in south-eastern Alabama, to John Silas Ziglar and Lila Wescott Ziglar. He was the tenth of 12 children.

46. **Unknown.**

47. **Unknown.**

48. **Unknown.**

49. **Unknown.**

50. **Unknown.**

51. **Aaron Koduah** is a former supply chain specialist in the British Army and holds a Bachelor's degree in Accounting and Business Management. Aaron is also a Professional and certified life coach helping individuals build their self-confidence.

52. **Christine Caine** is an Australian activist, evangelist, author, and international speaker. Caine and her husband, Nick are best known for founding The A21 Campaign in a non-profit, non-governmental organization that combats human trafficking.

53. **Anonymous.**

54. **Unknown.**

55. **Unknown.**

56. **J. K. Rowling** is a British novelist, philanthropist, film and television producer and screenwriter best known for writing the Harry Potter fantasy series. The books have won multiple awards, and sold more than 500 million copies becoming the best-selling book series in history.

57. **Franklin D. Roosevelt** was an American statesman and political leader who served as the 32nd President of the United States from 1933 until his death in 1945. A Democrat, he won a record four presidential elections and became a central figure in world events during the mid-20th century.

58. **Paulo Coelho** is a Brazilian lyricist and novelist and the recipient of numerous international awards. He is best known for his widely translated novel The Alchemist.

59. **Unknown.**

60. **Unknown.**

61. **Unknown.**

62. **Johnny Depp** is an American actor, producer, and musician. He has been nominated for three Academy Awards and has won the Golden Globe and Screen Actors Guild Awards for Best Actor. Depp rose to prominence on the 1980s television series 21 Jump Street, becoming a teen idol.

63. **Unknown.**

64. **Wayne Dyer** was an American philosopher, self-help author, and a motivational speaker. His first book, Your Erroneous Zones, is one of the best-selling books of all time, with an estimated 35 million copies sold to date.

65. **Unknown.**

66. **Joyce Meyer** is a Charismatic Christian author and speaker and president of Joyce Meyer Ministries. Meyer and her husband Dave have four grown children, and live outside St. Louis, Missouri.

67. **Unknown.**

68. **Unknown.**

69. **Unknown.**

70. **Ralph Marston** was a professional football player who spent a season in the National Football League with the Boston Bulldogs in 1929.

71. **Carl G. Jung** was a Swiss psychiatrist and psychoanalyst who founded analytical psychology. His work has been influential in not only psychiatry but also anthropology, archaeology, literature, philosophy, and religious studies.

72. **Unknown.**

73. **Elisabeth Kubler-ross** was a Swiss-American psychiatrist, a pioneer in near-death studies and the author of the ground breaking book On Death and Dying (1969), where she first

discussed her theory of the five stages of grief, also known as the Kübler-Ross model.

74. **Unknown.**

75. **Aaron Koduah** is a former supply chain specialist in the British Army and holds a Bachelor's degree in Accounting and Business Management. Aaron is also a Professional and certified life coach helping individuals build their self-confidence.

76. **Dr. Steve Maraboli** is a life-changing Speaker, bestselling Author and Behavioural Scientist who lends his popular voice to various topics.

77. **Hubert Humphrey** was an American politician who served as the 38th Vice President of the United States from 1965 to 1969. He twice served in the United States Senate, representing Minnesota from 1949 to 1964 and 1971 to 1978.

78. **Unknown.**

79. **Jenni Young** is an American film producer and photographer. As a producer, Young's first feature film, Loving Annabelle, stars Erin Kelly, Diane Gaidry and Kevin McCarthy, debuted at the prestigious Cinequest Film Festival in 2006; the film won the Audience Award and Best Actress Award at Outfest.

80. **Epictetus** was a Greek Stoic philosopher. He was born a slave at Hierapolis, Phrygia and lived in Rome until his banishment,

when he went to Nicopolis in north western Greece for the rest of his life.

81. **Oscar Wilde** was an Irish poet and playwright. After writing in different forms throughout the 1880s, he became one of London's most popular playwrights in the early 1890s.

82. **Anonymous.**

83. **Anonymous.**

84. **Anonymous.**

85. **Aaron Koduah** is a former supply chain specialist in the British Army and holds a Bachelor's degree in Accounting and Business Management. Aaron is also a Professional and certified life coach helping individuals build their self-confidence.

86. **Confucius** was a Chinese teacher, editor, politician and philosopher of the Spring and Autumn period of Chinese history.

87. **Chuck T. Falcon** is the author of Family Desk Reference to Psychology and Psychology Made Easy.

88. **Aaron Koduah** is a former supply chain specialist in the British Army and holds a Bachelor's degree in Accounting and Business Management. Aaron is also a Professional and certified life coach helping individuals build their self-confidence.

89. **Deepak Chopra** is an Indian-born American author, public speaker, alternative medicine advocate and a prominent figure in the New Age movement.

90. **Unknown.**

91. **Oren Harari** was a business professor at the University of San Francisco as well as an author of several management books including The Leadership Secrets of Colin Powell, a New York Times, Wall Street Journal and Bloomberg Businessweek bestseller.

92. **Unknown.**

93. **Unknown.**

94. **Robin Sharma** is a Canadian writer and motivational speaker known for his The Monk Who Sold His Ferrari book series. Sharma worked as a litigation lawyer until age 25, when he self-published Mega Living, a book on stress management and spirituality.

95. **Steve Jobs** was an American entrepreneur and business magnate. He was the chairman, chief executive officer (CEO), and a co-founder of Apple Inc., chairman and majority shareholder of Pixar, a member of The Walt Disney Company's board of directors following its acquisition of Pixar, and the founder, chairman, and CEO of NeXT.

96. **Lou Holtz** is a former American football player, coach, and

analyst. He served as the head football coach at The College of William & Mary.

97. Unknown.

98. Unknown.

99. Madeline L'Engle was an American writer who wrote young adult fiction, including A Wrinkle in Time and its sequels: A Wind in the Door, A Swiftly Tilting Planet, Many Waters and An Acceptable Time.

100. Unknown.

101. Aaron Koduah is a former supply chain specialist in the British Army and holds a Bachelor's degree in Accounting and Business Management. Aaron is also a Professional and certified life coach helping individuals build their self-confidence.

102. Bob Moawad was the owner of Edge Learning Institute and original creator of the Increasing Human Effectiveness program.

103. Unknown.

104. Unknown.

105. Mildred D. Taylor is an African-American writer known for her works exploring the struggle faced by African-American families in the Deep South. Taylor's most famous book is Roll of Thunder, Hear My Cry.

106. Unknown.

107. Unknown.

108. Unknown.

109. Robert Holden is a British psychologist, author and broadcaster who works in the field of positive psychology and well-being and is considered Britain's foremost expert on happiness.

110. Unknown.

111. Aaron Koduah is a former supply chain specialist in the British Army and holds a Bachelor's degree in Accounting and Business Management. Aaron is also a Professional and certified life coach helping individuals build their self-confidence.

112. Unknown.

113. Unknown.

114. Aaron Koduah is a former supply chain specialist in the British Army and holds a Bachelor's degree in Accounting and Business Management. Aaron is also a Professional and certified life coach helping individuals build their self-confidence.

115. Wale Ayeni leads the IFC's Venture Capital practice focused on Africa, South of the Sahara – the International Finance Organization is part of the World Bank Group. The IFC's

Venture capital team invests in technology companies in frontier markets and has $1BN AUM.

116. **Unknown.**

117. **Ann Landers** was an American advice columnist and eventually a nationwide media celebrity. She began writing the Ask Ann Landers column in 1955 and continued for 47 years. Ann Landers was a pen name for Esther Pauline.

118. **Unknown.**

119. **Unknown.**

120. **Unknown.**

121. **Charlie Chaplin** was an English comic actor, filmmaker, and composer who rose to fame in the era of silent film. Chaplin became a worldwide icon through his screen persona 'The Tramp' and is considered one of the most important figures in the history of the film industry.

122. **Unknown.**

123. **Unknown.**

124. **Unknown.**

125. **Unknown.**

126. **Unknown.**

127. **Dr. Seuss** was an American author, political cartoonist, poet, animator, book publisher and artist, best known for authoring

more than 60 children's books.

128. Rebecca Black is an American YouTuber and singer who gained extensive media coverage when the music video for her 2011 single "Friday" went viral on YouTube and other social media sites.

129. Unknown.

130. Unknown.

131. Unknown.

132. Unknown.

133. Unknown.

134. Unknown.

135. Marcus Aurelius was Roman emperor from 161 to 180. He ruled with his adoptive brother, Lucius Verus, until Verus' death in 169, and with his son, Commodus, from 177. He was the last of the so-called Five Good Emperors.

136. Oscar Wilde was an Irish poet and playwright. After writing in different forms throughout the 1880s, he became one of London's most popular playwrights in the early 1890s.

137. Unknown.

138. George Bernard Shaw was an Irish playwright, critic, polemicist, and political activist. His influence on Western theatre, culture and politics extended from the 1880s to his death and beyond.

139. Norman Vincent Peale was an American minister and author known for his work in popularizing the concept of positive thinking, especially through his best-selling book The Power of Positive Thinking.

140. Roy T. Bennett was chairman of the Ohio Republican Party, and one of three Ohio representatives to the Republican National Committee, of which he had been a member for more than two decades.

141. Unknown.

142. Unknown.

143. Maya Angelou was an American poet, singer, memoirist, and civil rights activist. She published seven autobiographies, three books of essays, several books of poetry, and was credited with a list of plays, movies, and television shows spanning over 50 years.

144. Unknown.

145. Unknown.

146. Unknown.

147. Les Brown is an American motivational speaker, author, radio DJ, former television host, and former politician. As a politician, he is a former member of the Ohio House of Representatives.

148. Helen Mirren is an English actor. Mirren began her acting career with the Royal Shakespeare Company in 1967 and is one of the few performers who have achieved the Triple Crown of Acting.

149. **Les Brown** is an American motivational speaker, author, radio DJ, former television host, and former politician. As a politician, he is a former member of the Ohio House of Representatives.

150. **Billy Cox** is an American bassist, best known for performing with Jimi Hendrix. Cox is the only surviving member of Jimi Hendrix's three main bands, including the original Experience line-up (which did not include Cox); he was in the Band of Gypsys and afterwards the Cry Of Love trio a.k.a. the Jimi Hendrix New Experience.

151. **Unknown.**

152. **Unknown.**

153. **Unknown.**

154. **Cassie Parks** is the author of Choose Me.

155. **Unknown.**

156. **Unknown.**

157. **Lao Tzu** was an ancient Chinese philosopher and writer. He is the reputed author of the Tao Te Ching, the founder of philosophical Taoism, and a deity in religious Taoism and traditional Chinese religions.

158. **Robert Hand** is an American astrologer, historian, author and scholar. He began studying astrology at the age of 17. His father, Wilfred Hand, was a specialist in Cosmo biology and heliocentric astrology, and used astrological charts to forecast changes in the stock market, and taught his son the basics of casting astrological charts.

159. **Carl Jung** was a Swiss psychiatrist and psychoanalyst who founded analytical psychology. His work has been influential in not only psychiatry but also anthropology, archaeology, literature, philosophy, and religious studies.

160. **Unknown.**

161. **Unknown.**

162. **Unknown.**

163. **Michael Josephson** is a former law professor and attorney who founded the non-profit Joseph and Edna Josephson Institute of Ethics located in Los Angeles, California, out of which he operates as a speaker and lecturer on the subject of ethics.

164. **Barrie Davenport** is the founder of BarrieDavenport.com and creator of the top-ranked personal development blog, Live Bold and Bloom.

165. **Dr. Robert Anthony** was an American organizational theorist, and professor of management control at Harvard Business School, known for his work in the field of

management control systems.

166. **Henry Ford** was an American captain of industry and a business magnate, the founder of the Ford Motor Company, and the sponsor of the development of the assembly line technique of mass production.

167. **Don Shula** is a former professional American football coach and player who is best known as the head coach of the Miami Dolphins, the team he led to two Super Bowl victories, and to the seasoning the history of the National Football League NFL.

168. **Unknown.**

169. **Unknown.**

170. **Thomas Carlyle** was a Scottish philosopher, satirical writer, essayist, translator, historian, mathematician, and teacher.

171. **Marilyn Monroe** was an American actress, model, and singer. Famous for playing comic "Blonde Bombshell" characters, she became one of the most popular sex symbols of the 1950s and was emblematic of the era's attitudes towards sexuality.

172. **Unknown.**

173. **Jason Pockrandt** is a Speaker and Life Coach who connects millennial fathers to their true selves by rediscovering who and what matters most. He is the author of Tear Your Box

Apart. A Manifesto on Freedom.

174. **Aaron Koduah** is a former supply chain specialist in the British Army and holds a Bachelor's degree in Accounting and Business Management. Aaron is also a Professional and certified life coach helping individuals build their self-confidence.

175. **Unknown.**

176. **Unknown.**

177. **Unknown.**

178. **Unknown.**

179. **Unknown.**

180. **Anonymous.**

181. **Harvey Fierstein** is an American actor, playwright, and voice actor. Fierstein has won the Tony Award for Best Actor in a Play for his own play Torch Song Trilogy about a gay drag-performer and his quest for true love and family and the Tony Award for Best Actor in a Musical for playing Edna Turnblad in Hairspray.

182. **Eleanor Roosevelt** was an American political figure, diplomat and activist. She served as the First Lady of the United States from March 1933 to April 1945 during her husband President Franklin D. Roosevelt's four terms in office, making her the longest serving First Lady of the

United States.

183. **Paul Tillich** was a German-American Christian existentialist philosopher and Lutheran Protestant theologian who is widely regarded as one of the most influential theologians of the twentieth century.

184. **Lao Tzu** was an ancient Chinese philosopher and writer. He is the reputed author of the Tao Te Ching, the founder of philosophical Taoism, and a deity in religious Taoism and traditional Chinese religions.

185. **Ralph Waldo Emerson** was an American essayist, lecturer, philosopher, and poet who led the transcendentalist movement of the mid-19th century.

186. **Albert Einstein** was a German-born theoretical physicist who developed the theory of relativity, one of the two pillars of modern physics. His work is also known for its influence on the philosophy of science.

187. **Elmer G. Letterman** was born on January 16, 1897, in Charlottesville, Virginia. He was the son of Jack J. Leterman and Bertie (Goldsmith) Leterman. Mr Leterman was the author of a number of best-selling books: The Sale Begins When the Customer Says No, Personal Power through Creative Selling and others.

188. **Ian Wallace** was an English bass-baritone opera and concert singer, actor and broadcaster of Scottish extraction. His

family intended him for a career in the law, but he was attracted to the stage.

189. Unknown.

190. Unknown.

191. Unknown.

192. Unknown.

193. Green Goblin is the alias of several fictional supervillains appearing in American comic books published by Marvel Comics.

194. Theodore Roosevelt was an American statesman and writer who served as the 26th President of the United States from 1901 to 1909.

195. Robert Morley was an English actor who was usually cast as a pompous English gentleman representing the Establishment, often in supporting roles.

196. Maxwell Maltz was an American cosmetic surgeon and author of Psycho-Cybernetics, which was a system of ideas that he claimed could improve one's self-image. In turn, the person would lead a more successful and fulfilling life.

197. Rob Liano is a Best-Selling Author, a Certified Life Coach, Public Speaker, and Blogger. Through logic, insight and humour, Rob Liano has brought a fresh perspective to Sales Training and Success Coaching.

198. Unknown.

199. Roger Ebert was an American film critic, historian, journalist, screenwriter, and author. He was a film critic for the Chicago Sun-Times from 1967 until his death in 2013.

200. Shannon L. Alder is an inspirational author. Her titbits of wisdom have been published in over 100 different books, by various relationship authors and in several online magazine articles (Psychology Today, Huffington Post, etc.).

201. Aaron Koduah is a former supply chain specialist in the British Army and holds a Bachelor's degree in Accounting and Business Management. Aaron is also a Professional and certified life coach helping individuals build their self-confidence.

202. Unknown.

203. Unknown.

204. Unknown.

205. Unknown.

206. Unknown.

207. Unknown.

208. Unknown.

209. Shanti Deva was born in Delhi, India. As a little girl in the 1930s she began to claim to remember details of a past life. The case was brought to the attention of Mahatma

Gandhi who set up a commission to investigate; a report was published in 1936.

210. Unknown.

211. Unknown.

212. Unknown.

213. Unknown.

214. Unknown.

215. **John Wooden** was an American basketball player and head coach at the University of California at Los Angeles.

216. **Anthony Robbins** is an American author, entrepreneur, philanthropist and life coach. Robbins is known for his infomercials, seminars, and self-help books including Unlimited Power and Awaken the Giant Within.

217. **Michael Le Boeuf** is an American business author and former management professor at the University of New Orleans.

218. **Andrew J. Bernstein** is an American philosopher. He is a proponent of Objectivism, the philosophy of Ayn Rand, and the author of several books, both fiction and non-fiction.

219. **Aaron Koduah** is a former supply chain specialist in the British Army and holds a Bachelor's degree in Accounting and Business Management. Aaron is also a Professional and certified life coach helping individuals build their self-confidence.

220. Unknown.

221. Katie Courtice is American Freelance writer and editor, office consultant. Member Editl. Freelancers Association.

222. Unknown.

223. Thelma Davis was one of the longest dancers of the original Soul Train gang and was the smoothest, coolest, and the most divine of the female dancers. She was a true definition of a dancer.

224. Unknown.

225. Unknown.

226. Ellen J. Langer is a professor of psychology at Harvard University; in 1981, she became the first woman ever to be tenured in psychology at Harvard. Langer studies the illusion of control, decision-making, aging, and mindfulness theory.

227. Rick Hanson is a psychologist and New York Times best-selling author. His books include Hardwiring Happiness, Buddha's.

228. Unknown.

229. Unknown.

230. Unknown.

231. Naval Ravikant is the CEO and a co-founder of AngelList. He previously co-founded Epinions which went public as part of Shopping.com and Vast.com.

232. **Robert Tew** has been Chairman at Newcastle Knights Limited since April 11, 2011 and its Director since April 2008. Mr. Tew served as Director of Tew Property Consultants. He was Committee Member of Once a Knight Old Boys Club Inc.

233. **Brian Tracy** is a Canadian-American motivational public speaker and self-development author. He is the author of over seventy books that have been translated into dozens of languages.

234. **Anonymous.**

235. **Lori Deschene** is the founder of the popular Tiny Buddha blog, she is an example of an introvert who has forged her own path.

236. **Marc and Angel** are a couple from the USA, they founded "Marc and Angel Hack Life" in 2006 with the goal of inspiring as many people as possible.

237. **Unknown.**

238. **Unknown.**

239. **Paulo Coelho** is a Brazilian lyricist and novelist and the recipient of numerous international awards. He is best known for his widely translated novel The Alchemist.

240. **Anonymous.**

241. **Unknown.**

242. **Erin Olivo** is an assistant clinical professor of medical psychology at the Columbia University College of Physicians and Surgeons. She helps patients dealing with stress, anxiety and depression. She is a mindfulness meditation expert.

243. **Unknown.**

244. **E. Joseph Cossman** was a door-to-door salesman who perfected mail-order salesmanship and pioneered the television infomercial, then wrote books and conducted pricey seminars to demonstrate the route from rags to riches,

245. **Unknown.**

246. **Unknown.**

247. **Tony Gaskins** is a motivational speaker, author and life coach. Having appeared on The Oprah Winfrey Show, The Tyra Banks Show and TBN's 700 Club.

248. **Unknown.**

249. **Unknown.**

250. **Mike Dooley** is a New York Times Bestselling author, speaker, and entrepreneur in the philosophical New Thought movement.

251. **Dr. Denis Waitley** is an American motivational speaker, writer and consultant. He has been recognized as the best-selling author of the audio series, The Psychology of Winning and books such as "Seeds of Greatness" and "The

Winner's Edge". Waitley has been inducted into the International Speakers' Hall of Fame.

252. **Unknown.**

253. **Dr. Steve Maraboli** is a life-changing Speaker, bestselling Author, and Behavioural Scientist who lends his popular voice to various topics.

254. **Unknown.**

255. **Unknown.**

256. **Unknown.**

257. **Unknown.**

258. **Henry Cloud** is an American Christian self-help author. Cloud co-authored Boundaries: When to Say Yes, How to Say No to Take Control of Your Life in 1992 which sold two million copies and evolved into a five-part series.

259. **Unknown.**

260. **Zig Ziglar** was an American author, salesman, and motivational speaker. Zig Ziglar was born in Coffee County in south-eastern Alabama, to John Silas Ziglar and Lila Wescott Ziglar. He was the tenth of 12 children.

261. **George Bernard Shaw** was an Irish playwright, critic, polemicist, and political activist. His influence on Western theatre, culture and politics extended from the 1880s to his death and beyond.

262. **Unknown.**

263. **Jim Rohn** was an American entrepreneur, author and motivational speaker.

264. **Charles Darwin** was an English naturalist, geologist and biologist, best known for his contributions to the science of evolution.

265. **Unknown.**

266. **Max De Pree** was an American businessman and writer. A son of D. J. De Pree, founder of Herman Miller office furniture company, he and his brother Hugh De Pree assumed leadership of the company in the early 1960s, Hugh becoming CEO and president in 1962.

267. **Albert Einstein** was a German-born theoretical physicist who developed the theory of relativity, one of the two pillars of modern physics. His work is also known for its influence on the philosophy of science.

268. **Carl Bard** is a leading multinational developer, manufacturer, and marketer of medical technologies in the fields of vascular, urology, oncology, and surgical specialties.

269. **Viktor E. Frankl** was an Austrian neurologist and psychiatrist as well as a Holocaust survivor. Frankl was the founder of logotherapy, which is a form of existential analysis, the "Third Viennese School of Psychotherapy".

270. **Hugh Prather** was an American self-help writer, lay minister, and counsellor, most famous for his first book, Notes to Myself, which was first published in 1970 by Real People Press, and later reprinted by Bantam Books.

271. **Arnold Bennett** was an English writer. He is best known as a novelist, but he also worked in other fields such as the theatre, journalism, propaganda and films.

272. **Unknown.**

273. **Unknown.**

274. **Unknown.**

275. **Stephen Fry** is an English comedian, actor, writer, presenter, and activist. With Hugh Laurie, he is half of the comic double act Fry and Laurie, who starred in A Bit of Fry & Laurie and Jeeves and Wooster.

276. **John Lilly** was an American physician, neuroscientist, psychoanalyst, psychonaut, philosopher, writer and inventor.

277. **Unknown.**

278. **Unknown.**

279. **Unknown.**

280. **Jim Rohn** was an American entrepreneur, author and motivational speaker.

281. **Unknown.**

282. **Jon Kabat-Zin** is an American professor emeritus of medicine and the creator of the Stress Reduction Clinic and the Centre for Mindfulness in Medicine, Health Care, and Society at the University of Massachusetts Medical School.

283. **Andy Warhol** was an American artist, director and producer who was a leading figure in the visual art movement known as pop art.

284. **Unknown.**

285. **Mandy Hale** is the Author of a book known as: The Single Woman which is widely recognized around the world.

286. **Jim Rohn** was an American entrepreneur, author and motivational speaker.

287. **Mary Engelbreit** is a graphic artist and children's book illustrator who launched her own magazine, Mary Engelbreit's Home Companion in 1996. Mary Engelbreit was born in St. Louis, Missouri.

288. **Unknown.**

289. **Unknown.**

290. **Unknown.**

291. **John F. Kennedy** was an American politician who served as the 35th President of the United States from January 1961 until his assassination in November 1963.

292. **Unknown.**

293. **John F. Kennedy** was an American politician who served as the 35th President of the United States from January 1961 until his assassination in November 1963.

294. **Denis Waitley** is an American motivational speaker, writer and consultant. He has been recognized as the best-selling author of the audio series, The Psychology of Winning and books such as "Seeds of Greatness" and The Winner's Edge. Waitley has been inducted into the International Speakers' Hall of Fame.

295. **Dalai Lama** is the current Dalai Lama. Dalai Lamas are important monks of the Gelug school, the newest school of Tibetan Buddhism which was formally headed by the Ganden Tripas.

296. **Unknown.**

297. **Unknown.**

298. **Unknown.**

299. **Denzel Washington** is an American actor, director, and producer. He has received three Golden Globe awards, a Tony Award, and two Academy Awards: Best Supporting Actor for the historical war drama film Glory (1989) and Best Actor for his role as a corrupt cop in the crime thriller Training Day (2001).

300. **Unknown.**

301. **Earl Nightingale** was an American radio speaker and author, dealing mostly with the subjects of human character development, motivation, and meaningful existence.

302. **Albert Einstein** was a German-born theoretical physicist who developed the theory of relativity, one of the two pillars of modern physics. His work is also known for its influence on the philosophy of science.

303. **Karen Lamb** is the author of Thea Astley: Inventing Her Own Weather, which made the Queensland Literary Awards 2015 shortlist in the category of Nonfiction.

304. **Aaron Koduah** is a former supply chain specialist in the British Army and holds a Bachelor's degree in Accounting and Business Management. Aaron is also a Professional and certified life coach helping individuals build their self-confidence.

305. **Les Brown** is an American motivational speaker, author, radio DJ, former television host, and former politician. As a politician, he is a former member of the Ohio House of Representatives.

306. **Confucius** was a Chinese teacher, editor, politician, and philosopher of the Spring and Autumn period of Chinese history.

307. **Bobby Knight** is a retired American basketball coach. Nicknamed 'The General', Knight won 902 NCAA Division

I men's college basketball games, the most all-time at the time of his retirement.

308. Tony Gaskins Jr. is a motivational speaker, author and life coach. Having appeared on The Oprah Winfrey Show, The Tyra Banks Show and TBN's 700 Club.

309. Unknown.

310. Mark Victor Hansen is an American inspirational and motivational speaker, trainer and author. He is best known as the founder and co-creator of the "Chicken Soup for the Soul" book series.

311. Osho was an Indian godman and leader of the Rajneesh movement. During his lifetime he was viewed as a controversial new religious movement leader and mystic.

312. Stephen Covey was an American educator, author, businessman, and keynote speaker. His most popular book is 'The 7 Habits of Highly Effective People'.

313. Bruce Lee was a Hong Kong and American actor, film director, martial artist, martial arts instructor, philosopher, and founder of the martial art Jeet Kune Do, one of the wushu or Kungfu styles.

314. William Barclay was a Scottish author, radio and television presenter, Church of Scotland minister and Professor of Divinity and Biblical Criticism at the University of Glasgow.

315. **Bill Gates** is an American business magnate, investor, author, philanthropist, humanitarian, and principal founder of Microsoft Corporation.

316. **Bill Cosby** is an American stand-up comedian, actor, musician, author, and convicted sex offender. Bill Cosby began his career as a stand-up comic at the hungry I in San Francisco during the 1960s.

317. **Anthony Robbins** is an American author, entrepreneur, philanthropist and life coach. Robbins is known for his infomercials, seminars, and self-help books including Unlimited Power and Awaken the Giant Within.

318. **Larry McMurtry** is an American novelist, essayist, bookseller, and screenwriter whose work is predominantly set in either the Old West or in contemporary Texas.

319. **George Elliot** was an English novelist, poet, journalist, translator, and one of the leading writers of the Victorian era.

320. **Paulo Coelho** is a Brazilian lyricist and novelist and the recipient of numerous international awards. He is best known for his widely translated novel The Alchemist.

321. **Kevin Ngo** is the owner of MotivationalWellBeing.com, a motivation website full of resources that attracts several hundred thousand visitors a month. His knowledge comes from studying the field of personal development for the past 15 years.

322. Dr. Steve Maraboli is a life-changing Speaker, bestselling Author, and Behavioural Scientist who lends his popular voice to various topics.

323. Paulo Coelho is a Brazilian lyricist and novelist and the recipient of numerous international awards. He is best known for his widely translated novel The Alchemist.

324. Unknown.

325. Odille Rault is an author, inspirational speaker and life coach who specializes in helping readers and clients to empower themselves through developing unconditional love for themselves and others.

326. Unknown.

327. Herman Cain is an American politician and author, business executive, radio host, syndicated columnist, and Tea Party activist from Georgia. He was a candidate for the 2012 U.S. Republican Party presidential nomination.

328. David Brooks is an American author and conservative political and cultural commentator who writes for The New York Times. He has worked as a film critic for The Washington Times; a reporter and later op-ed editor for The Wall Street Journal.

329. Abraham Lincoln was an American statesman and lawyer who served as the 16th President of the United States from March 1861 until his assassination in April 1865.

330. **Oprah Winfrey** is an American media proprietor, talk show host, actress, producer, and philanthropist.

331. **Vince Lombardi** was an American football player, coach, and executive in the National Football League.

332. **Oliver W. Holmes** was an American jurist who served as an Associate Justice of the Supreme Court of the United States from 1902 to 1932, and as Acting Chief Justice of the United States from January–February 1930.

333. **Buddha** also known as Siddhartha Gautama, Shakyamuni Buddha, or simply the Buddha, after the title of Buddha, was an ascetic and sage, on whose teachings Buddhism was founded.

334. **Ralph Waldo Emerson** was an American essayist, lecturer, philosopher, and poet who led the transcendentalist movement of the mid-19th century.

335. **Randy Pausch** was an American professor of computer science, human–computer interaction, and design at Carnegie Mellon University in Pittsburgh, Pennsylvania.

336. **Albert Einstein** was a German-born theoretical physicist who developed the theory of relativity, one of the two pillars of modern physics. His work is also known for its influence on the philosophy of science.

337. **Unknown.**

338. **Zig Ziglar** was an American author, salesman, and motivational speaker. Zig Ziglar was born in Coffee County in south-eastern Alabama, to John Silas Ziglar and Lila Wescott Ziglar. He was the tenth of 12 children.

339. **Kevin Ngo** is the owner of MotivationalWellBeing.com, a motivation website full of resources that attracts several hundred thousand visitors a month. His knowledge comes from studying the field of personal development for the past 15 years.

340. **John C. Maxwell** is an American author, speaker, and pastor who has written many books, primarily focusing on leadership. Titles include 'The 21 Irrefutable Laws of Leadership' and 'The 21 Indispensable Qualities of a Leader'.

341. **Martin Luther King Jr.** was an American Baptist minister and activist who became the most visible spokesperson and leader in the civil rights movement from 1954 until his death in 1968.

342. **Kevin Ngo** is the owner of MotivationalWellBeing.com, a motivation website full of resources that attracts several hundred thousand visitors a month. His knowledge comes from studying the field of personal development for the past 15 years.

343. **Michael Jordan** is an American former professional basketball player. He played 15 seasons in the National

Basketball Association for the Chicago Bulls and Washington Wizards.

344. **Joe Tichio** is an actor, known for A Happy Ending (2005), Life, Love, & Hollywood (2008) and Gamers (2001).

345. **Michael Masterson** is an American author, entrepreneur, publisher, real estate investor, filmmaker, art collector, and consultant to the direct marketing and publishing industries.

346. **Steven Hayes** is a clinical psychologist and Nevada Foundation Professor at the University of Nevada, Reno Department of Psychology, where he runs the leading Ph.D. program in Behaviour Analysis and coined the term Clinical Behaviour Analysis.

347. **Akio Morita** was a Japanese businessman and co-founder of Sony along with Masaru Ibuka.

348. **Henry David Thoreau** was an American essayist, poet, philosopher, abolitionist, naturalist, tax resister, development critic, surveyor, and historian.

349. **R. Kelly** is an American singer, songwriter, record producer, and former professional basketball player. A native of Chicago, Kelly began performing during the late 1980s and debuted in 1992 with the group Public Announcement.

350. **Alice Walker** is an American novelist, short story writer, poet, and activist. She wrote the novel The Colour Purple, for which she won the National Book Award for hardcover

fiction, and the Pulitzer Prize for Fiction.

351. Arnold Schwarzenegger is an Austrian-American actor, director, filmmaker, businessman, investor, author, philanthropist, activist, politician, and former professional bodybuilder and powerlifter.

352. Anonymous.

353. Unknown.

354. Martin Luther King Jr. was an American Baptist minister and activist who became the most visible spokesperson and leader in the civil rights movement from 1954 until his death in 1968.

355. Anonymous.

356. Aaron Koduah is a former supply chain specialist in the British Army and holds a Bachelor's degree in Accounting and Business Management. Aaron is also a Professional and certified life coach helping individuals build their self-confidence.

357. Unknown.

358. Unknown.

359. Earl Nightingale was an American radio speaker and author, dealing mostly with the subjects of human character development, motivation, and meaningful existence.

360. Unknown.

361. **Aaron Koduah** is a former supply chain specialist in the British Army and holds a Bachelor's degree in Accounting and Business Management. Aaron is also a Professional and certified life coach helping individuals build their self-confidence.

362. **Arthur Ashe** was an American professional tennis player who won three Grand Slam titles. Ashe was the first black player selected to the United States Davis Cup team and the only black man ever to win the singles title at Wimbledon,

363. **Aaron Koduah** is a former supply chain specialist in the British Army and holds a Bachelor's degree in Accounting and Business Management. Aaron is also a Professional and certified life coach helping individuals build their self-confidence.

364. **Unknown.**

365. **Gretchen Rubin** is an American author, blogger and speaker. Rubin is a writer on subjects of habits, happiness, and human nature. She is the author of the New York Times bestsellers Better Than Before, Happier at Home and The Happiness Project.

366. **Jim Rohn** was an American entrepreneur, author and motivational speaker.

367. **Muhammad Ali** was an American professional boxer, activist, and philanthropist. He is widely regarded as one of

the most significant and celebrated sports figures of the 20th century.

368. **Napoleon Hill** was an American self-help author. He is known best for his book Think and Grow Rich which is among the 10 bestselling self-help books of all time.

369. **Anthony Robbins** is an American author, entrepreneur, philanthropist and life coach. Robbins is known for his infomercials, seminars, and self-help books including Unlimited Power and Awaken the Giant Within.

370. **Thomas Edison** was an American inventor and businessman, who has been described as America's greatest inventor.

371. **Bruce Lee** was a Hong Kong and American actor, film director, martial artist, martial arts instructor, philosopher, and founder of the martial art Jeet Kune Do, one of the wushu or Kungfu styles.

372. **Vince Lombardi** was an American football player, coach, and executive in the National Football League.

373. **Confucius** was a Chinese teacher, editor, politician, and philosopher of the Spring and Autumn period of Chinese history.

374. **Doug Firebaugh** is an Author, Radio Talk Show Host, Success, Leadership, and Home Business Trainer MLM Network Marketing Consultant.

375. Albert Einstein was a German-born theoretical physicist who developed the theory of relativity, one of the two pillars of modern physics. His work is also known for its influence on the philosophy of science.

376. Joshua J. Marine is an author and particularly famous for his quotes. His accomplishments might include that his quotes are selected by many websites as quote of the day.

377. Unknown.

378. Unknown.

379. Unknown.

380. Unknown.

381. Abraham Lincoln was an American statesman and lawyer who served as the 16th President of the United States from March 1861 until his assassination in April 1865.

382. Unknown.

383. Unknown.

384. Muhammad Ali was an American professional boxer, activist, and philanthropist. He is widely regarded as one of the most significant and celebrated sports figures of the 20th century.

385. Unknown.

386. Aaron Koduah is a former supply chain specialist in the British Army and holds a Bachelor's degree in Accounting and Business Management. Aaron is also a Professional and certified life coach helping individuals build their self-confidence.

387. **Unknown.**

388. **Jim Rohn** was an American entrepreneur, author and motivational speaker.

389. **Unknown.**

390. **Winston Churchill** was a British politician, army officer, and writer, who was Prime Minister of the United Kingdom from 1940 to 1945 and again from 1951 to 1955.

391. **Ramana Maharshi** was a Hindu sage and jivanmukta. He was born as Venkataraman Iyer but is most commonly known by the name Bhagavan Sri Ramana Maharshi. He was born in what is now Tiruchuli, Tamil Nadu, India.

392. **Tommy Lasorda** is a former Major League Baseball pitcher who is best known for his two decades as manager of the Los Angeles Dodgers.

393. **Thomas Fowell Buxton** was an English Member of Parliament, brewer, abolitionist and social reformer. He had connections with the Gurney family.

394. **Helen Keller** was an American author, political activist, and lecturer. She was the first deaf-blind person to earn a Bachelor of Arts degree.

395. Michael Jordan is an American former professional basketball player. He played 15 seasons in the National Basketball Association for the Chicago Bulls and Washington Wizards.

396. Lou Holtz is a former American football player, coach, and analyst. Holtz is the only college football coach to lead six different programs to bowl games and the only coach to guide four different programs to the final top 20 rankings.

397. Ralph Waldo Emerson was an American essayist, lecturer, philosopher, and poet who led the transcendentalist movement of the mid-19th century.

398. Unknown.

399. Confucius was a Chinese teacher, editor, politician, and philosopher of the Spring and Autumn period of Chinese history.

400. Marilyn Monroe was an American actress, model, and singer. Famous for playing comic "Blonde Bombshell" characters, she became one of the most popular sex symbols of the 1950s and was emblematic of the era's attitudes towards sexuality.

401. Elbert Hubbard was an American writer, publisher, artist, and philosopher. Raised in Hudson, Illinois, he had early success as a traveling salesman for the Larkin Soap Company.

402. Unknown.

403. **Maya Angelou** was an American poet, singer, memoirist, and civil rights activist. She published seven autobiographies, three books of essays, several books of poetry, and was credited with a list of plays, movies, and television shows spanning over 50 years.

404. **Jodi Picoult** is an American writer. She was awarded the New England Bookseller Award for fiction in 2003. Currently approximately 14 million copies of her books are in print worldwide, translated into 34 languages.

405. **Unknown.**

406. **Unknown.**

407. **Paulo Coelho** is a Brazilian lyricist and novelist and the recipient of numerous international awards. He is best known for his widely translated novel The Alchemist.

408. **Dr. Steve Maraboli** is a life-changing Speaker, bestselling Author, and Behavioural Scientist who lends his popular voice to various topics.

409. **Andre Dubus** was an American short story writer and essayist. Throughout his career, he published most of his work in small, distinguished literary journals such as Ploughshares and Sewanee Review.

410. **W. Clement Stone** was a businessman, philanthropist and New Thought self-help book author.

411. Unknown.

412. David Icke is an English writer and public speaker. A former footballer and sports broadcaster, Icke has been known since the 1990s as a professional conspiracy theorist.

413. Unknown.

414. English Proverb

415. Unknown.

416. Unknown.

417. Wayne Dyer was an American philosopher, self-help author, and a motivational speaker. His first book, Your Erroneous Zones, is one of the best-selling books of all time, with an estimated 35 million copies sold to date.

418. Unknown.

419. Joan Baez is an American singer, songwriter, musician, and activist whose contemporary folk music often includes songs of protest or social justice.

420. Unknown.

421. Seth Godin is an American author and former dot com business executive.

422. Unknown.

423. Unknown.

424. Khalil Gibran was a Lebanese-American writer, poet and visual artist. Gibran was born in the town of Bsharri in the Mount Lebanon Mutasarrifate, Ottoman Empire (modern day Lebanon), to Khalil Gibran and Kamila Gibran.

425. Unknown.

426. Unknown.

427. Leon Brown is a Welsh international rugby union player who plays for the Dragons regional team as a prop forward having previously played for Cross Keys RFC.

428. Unknown.

429. Unknown.

430. Unknown.

431. Unknown.

432. Unknown.

433. Unknown.

434. Allan Watts was a British philosopher who interpreted and popularised Eastern philosophy for a Western audience. Born in Chislehurst, England, he moved to the United States in 1938 and began Zen training in New York.

435. Unknown.

436. Unknown.

437. Unknown.

438. Dale Carnegie was an American writer and lecturer and the developer of famous courses in self-improvement, salesmanship, corporate training, public speaking, and interpersonal skills.

439. **Renee Jain** is one of the nation's most respected childhood happiness and resilience experts. She uses her many talents, specialized education, and business acumen in pursuit of her life's mission: To provide whole-brain education to children three years of age and older, regardless of where they live or of their families' socioeconomic background.

440. **Unknown.**

441. **Unknown.**

442. **Unknown.**

443. **Unknown.**

444. **Haddon W. Robinson** was the Harold John Ockenga Distinguished Professor of Preaching, senior director of the Doctor of Ministry program, and former interim President at Gordon-Conwell Theological Seminary.

445. **John Mayer-** is an American singer-songwriter, guitarist, and producer. Born in Bridgeport, Connecticut, Mayer attended Berklee College of Music in Boston, but disenrolled and moved to Atlanta in 1997 with Clay Cook.

446. **Roy T. Bennett** was chairman of the Ohio Republican Party, and one of three Ohio representatives to the Republican

National Committee, of which he had been a member for more than two decades.

447. **Ana Monnar** is the founder and president of Readers Are Leaders U.S.A., Inc. established in 2002. Lulu is the Yorkie rescue and family member, featured in Ana Monnar's registered trademark Readers Are Leaders U.S.A.

448. **Byron Pulsifer** is a retired criminologist, former manager of an employee assistance program, project manager and strategic planner, motivational speaker and motivational seminar leader.

449. **Ralph Waldo Emerson** was an American essayist, lecturer, philosopher, and poet who led the transcendentalist movement of the mid-19th century.

450. **Unknown.**

451. **Unknown.**

452. **Unknown.**

453. **Unknown.**

454. **Unknown.**

455. **Ambrose Bierce** was an American short story writer, journalist, poet, and Civil War veteran.

456. **Will Rogers** was a stage and motion picture actor, vaudeville performer, American cowboy, humourist, newspaper columnist, and social commentator from Oklahoma.

457. Dr. Steve Maraboli is a life-changing Speaker, bestselling Author, and Behavioural Scientist who lends his popular voice to various topics.

458. Buddha also known as Siddhartha Gautama, Shakyamuni Buddha, or simply the Buddha, after the title of Buddha, was an ascetic and sage, on whose teachings Buddhism was founded.

459. Unknown.

460. Aristotle was an ancient Greek philosopher and scientist born in the city of Stagira, Chalkidiki, in the north of Classical Greece.

461. Unknown.

462. Unknown.

463. Unknown.

464. Buddha also known as Siddhartha Gautama, Shakyamuni Buddha, or simply the Buddha, after the title of Buddha, was an ascetic and sage, on whose teachings Buddhism was founded.

465. Confucius was a Chinese teacher, editor, politician, and philosopher of the Spring and Autumn period of Chinese history.

466. Unknown.

467. Stephen Hawking was an English theoretical physicist, cosmologist, and author, who was director of research at the Centre for Theoretical Cosmology at the University of Cambridge at the time of his death.

468. **Evan Esar** was an American humourist who wrote Esar's Comic Dictionary in 1943, Humorous English in 1961, and 20,000 Quips and Quotes in 1968.

469. **Mother Teresa** known in the Roman Catholic Church as Saint Teresa of Calcutta, was an Albanian-Indian Roman Catholic nun and missionary. She was born in Skopje, then part of the Kosovo Vilayet of the Ottoman Empire.

470. **Unknown.**

471. **Unknown.**

472. **Unknown.**

473. **Harriet Nelson** was an American singer and actress. Nelson is best known for her role on the sitcom The Adventures of Ozzie and Harriet.

474. **Martin Luther King Jr.** was an American Baptist minister and activist who became the most visible spokesperson and leader in the civil rights movement from 1954 until his death in 1968.

475. **Unknown.**

476. **Plato** was a philosopher in Classical Greece and the founder of the Academy in Athens, the first institution of higher

learning in the Western world.

477. **Lawrence Douglas Wilder** is an American lawyer and politician who served as the 66th Governor of Virginia, from 1990 to 1994.

478. **Bruce Lee** was a Hong Kong and American actor, film director, martial artist, martial arts instructor, philosopher, and founder of the martial art Jeet Kune Do, one of the wushu or Kungfu styles.

479. **Robert Brault** is an American operatic tenor. Born in Michigan, he holds a B.M. degree from St. Norbert College from which he received a distinguished alumni award in 1997.

480. **Cherie Carter-Scott** is a No.1 New York Times Best Selling author. and Master Certified Executive and life coach.

481. **Eckhart Tolle** is a spiritual teacher. He is a German-born resident of Canada best known as the author of The Power of Now and A New Earth: Awakening to Your Life's Purpose.

482. **Unknown.**

483. **Unknown.**

484. **Unknown.**

485. **Unknown.**

486. **Lewis B. Smedes** was a renowned Christian author, ethicist, and theologian in the Reformed tradition. He was a professor

of theology and ethics for twenty-five years at Fuller Theological Seminary in Pasadena, California.

487. **Bryant H. McGill** is a Wall Street Journal and USA Today bestselling author, speaker, and activist in the fields of human potential and human rights.

488. **Bernard Meltzer** was a United States radio host for several decades. His advice call-in show, What's Your Problem? aired from 1967 until the mid-1990s on stations WCAU-AM and WPEN-AM in Philadelphia.

489. **Unknown.**

490. **Nelson Mandela** was a South African anti-apartheid revolutionary, political leader, and philanthropist, who served as President of South Africa from 1994 to 1999.

491. **Martin Luther King Jr.** was an American Baptist minister and activist who became the most visible spokesperson and leader in the civil rights movement from 1954 until his death in 1968.

492. **Kahlil Gibran** was a Lebanese-American writer, poet and visual artist. Gibran was born in the town of Bsharri in the Mount Lebanon Mutasarrifate, Ottoman Empire (modern day Lebanon), to Khalil Gibran and Kamila Gibran.

493. **Robert Enright** is a professor of educational psychology at the University of Wisconsin-Madison, a licensed psychologist, and the founding board member of the

International Forgiveness Institute, Inc.

494. **Mahatma Gandhi** was an Indian activist who was the leader of the Indian independence movement against British rule.

495. **Unknown.**

496. **Leon Brown** is a Welsh international rugby union player who plays for the Dragons regional team as a prop forward having previously played for Cross Keys RFC.

497. **Yolanda Hadid** is a Dutch-American television personality and former model. She is best known as a star of the American reality-television show The Real Housewives of Beverly Hills. She is mother to models Gigi Hadid, Bella Hadid, and Anwar Hadid.

498. **Martin Luther King Jr.** was an American Baptist minister and activist who became the most visible spokesperson and leader in the civil rights movement from 1954 until his death in 1968.

499. **Desmond Tutu** is a South African Anglican cleric and theologian known for his work as an anti-apartheid and human rights activist.

500. **Unknown.**

Printed in Great Britain
by Amazon